PENNSYLVANIA

Alpha

Warren

WORTHINGTON S.F.

BULL'S ISLAND S.P.

Merrill Creek Reservoir

Hunterdon

Spruce Run Reservoir

Round Valley Reservoir

COLD BROOK RES.

Sussex

STOKES S.F.

WALLKILL RIVER N.W.R.

HIGH POINT S.P.

Mercer

Trenton

HAMILTON-TRENTON.

Princeton

Mercer County Lake

ASSUNPINK W.M.A.

DUKE FARMS

NEGRI-NEPOTE NATIVE GRASSLAND PRES.

Six Mile Run Reservoir

Somerset

GLENHURST MEADOWS.

MORRISTOWN N.H.P.•
N.J. BRIG. AREA

SCHERMAN HOFFMAN
WILDLIFE SANC.

GREAT SWAMP N.W.R.

Morris

TROY MEADOWS
WETLANDS

RIFLE CAMP PARK.

MILLS RES.

Paterson

Passaic

VERNON CROSSING MARSH

Oradell Reservoir

NEW YORK

New Brunswick

Middlesex

Union

Newark

Essex

KEARNY MARSH.

MEADOWLANDS.

Bergen

GARRET MOUNTAIN RES.

Monmouth

Shark R.

Asbury Park

Elizabeth

Raritan
Bay

Sandy
Hook
Bay

GATEWAY N.R.A.

LIBERTY S.P.

Jersey City

Hudson

FORT LEE
HIST. PARK.

NEW YORK

NEW YORK /
NEW JERSEY
BIGHT

MW00477526

American Birding Association

Field Guide

to Birds of

New Jersey

Rick Wright

PHOTOGRAPHS BY
Brian E. Small
and Others

Scott & Nix, Inc.
NEW YORK

A SCOTT & NIX EDITION

COPYRIGHT © 2014 BY SCOTT & NIX, INC.
ALL RIGHTS RESERVED.

PUBLISHED BY
SCOTT & NIX, INC.
150 W 28TH ST, STE 1900
NEW YORK, NY 10001
SCOTTANDNIX.COM

FIRST EDITION 2014

ISBN 978-1-935622-42-0

AMERICAN BIRDING ASSOCIATION® AND ITS LOGO
ARE REGISTERED TRADEMARKS OF
THE AMERICAN BIRDING ASSOCIATION, INC.
ALL RIGHTS RESERVED.

AMERICAN BIRDING ASSOCIATION, INC.
800-850-2473
ABA.ORG

SCOTT & NIX, INC. BOOKS
ARE DISTRIBUTED TO THE TRADE BY:

INDEPENDENT PUBLISHERS GROUP (IPG)
814 NORTH FRANKLIN STREET
CHICAGO, IL 60610
800-888-4741
IPGBOOK.COM

PRINTED IN CHINA

Contents

The American Birding Association inspires all people to enjoy and protect wild birds.

The ABA represents the North American birding community and supports birders through publications, conferences, workshops, events, partnerships, and networks.

The ABA's education programs promote birding skills, ornithological knowledge, and the development of and implementation of a conservation ethic.

The ABA encourages birders to apply their skills to help conserve birds and their habitats, and we represent the interests of birders in planning and legislative arenas.

We welcome all birders as members.

THE AMERICAN BIRDING ASSOCIATION
CODE OF ETHICS

Everyone who enjoys birds and birding must always respect wildlife, its environment, and the rights of others. In any conflict of interest between birds and birders, the welfare of the birds and their environment comes first.

CODE OF BIRDING ETHICS

1. Promote the welfare of birds and their environment.

   1(a) Support the protection of important bird habitat.

   1(b) To avoid stressing birds or exposing them to danger, exercise restraint and caution during observation, photography, sound recording, or filming.

Limit the use of recordings and other methods of attracting birds, and never use such methods in heavily birded areas, or for attracting any species that is Threatened, Endangered, or of Special Concern, or is rare in your local area; Keep well back from nests and nesting colonies, roosts, display areas, and important feeding sites. In such sensitive areas, if there is a need for extended observation, photography, filming, or recording, try to use a blind or hide, and take advantage of natural cover.

Use artificial light sparingly for filming or photography, especially for close-ups.

1(c) Before advertising the presence of a rare bird, evaluate the potential for disturbance to the bird, its surroundings, and other people in the area, and proceed only if access can be controlled, disturbance minimized, and permission has been obtained from private land-owners. The sites of rare nesting birds should be divulged only to the proper conservation authorities.

1(d) Stay on roads, trails, and paths where they exist; otherwise keep habitat disturbance to a minimum.

2. Respect the law, and the rights of others.

2(a) Do not enter private property without the owner's explicit permission.

2(b) Follow all laws, rules, and regulations governing use of roads and public areas, both at home and abroad.

2(c) Practice common courtesy in contacts with other people. Your exemplary behavior will generate goodwill with birders and non-birders alike.

3. Ensure that feeders, nest structures, and other artificial bird environments are safe.

3(a) Keep dispensers, water, and food clean, and free of decay or disease. It is important to feed birds continually during harsh weather.

3(b) Maintain and clean nest structures regularly.

3(c) If you are attracting birds to an area, ensure the birds are not exposed to predation from cats and other domestic animals, or dangers posed by artificial hazards.

4. Group birding, whether organized or impromptu, requires special care.

Each individual in the group, in addition to the obligations spelled out in Items 1 and 2, has responsibilities as a Group Member.

4(a) Respect the interests, rights, and skills of fellow birders, as well as people participating in other legitimate outdoor activities. Freely share your knowledge and experience, except where code 1(c) applies. Be especially helpful to beginning birders.

4(b) If you witness unethical birding behavior, assess the situation, and intervene if you think it prudent. When interceding, inform the person(s) of the inappropriate action, and attempt, within reason, to have it stopped. If the behavior continues, document it, and notify appropriate individuals or organizations.

Group Leader Responsibilities [amateur and professional trips and tours].

4(c) Be an exemplary ethical role model for the group. Teach through word and example.

4(d) Keep groups to a size that limits impact on the environment, and does not interfere with others using the same area.

4(e) Ensure everyone in the group knows of and practices this code.

4(f) Learn and inform the group of any special circumstances applicable to the areas being visited (e.g. no tape recorders allowed).

4(g) Acknowledge that professional tour companies bear a special responsibility to place the welfare of birds and the benefits of public knowledge ahead of the company's commercial interests. Ideally, leaders should keep track of tour sightings, document unusual occurrences, and submit records to appropriate organizations.

Everyone who enjoys birds and birding must always respect wildlife, its environment, and the rights of others. The ABA Code of Ethics should be read, followed, and shared by all birders.

Please follow this code and distribute and teach it to others.

The American Birding Association's Code of Birding Ethics may be freely reproduced for distribution/dissemination. An electronic version may be found at www.aba.org/about/ethics.

Foreword

This may look like just a bird guide that you hold in your hands, if an exceptionally attractive and well-designed one. But let me assure you that it is far more than a book about the birds of New Jersey. Used well, it can be the start of a lifetime of enjoyment of birds in a state where the diversity of avian and other natural riches will astound you, as it has astounded me over the last four decades.

The great thing is that this book, like all the guides in this series, can help you do whatever you want with birding. Perhaps you enjoy birds a few days a year in your yard or local park and just want to know a little more about their ways and their world and be able to recall some of their names. Or maybe you want to dive deeper and really get familiar with the many amazing birds that inhabit the Garden State for part or all of each year.

Birding New Jersey, however you do it, will also lead you to meet some truly wonderful people. Rick Wright, who penned this handsome little book, is a prime example. Rick combines an absolutely stunning knowledge of birds and birding with patience and determination to present information in a way which others will find helpful and illuminating. And while Rick's combination of talents is certainly rare, you'll find that birders as a group are typically intelligent, passionate, and happy to share the excitement of birding.

I invite you to visit the American Birding Association website (www.aba.org), where you'll find a wealth of free resources and ways to connect with the birding community that will also help you get the most from your birding in New Jersey and beyond.

Now get on out there! Enjoy this book. Enjoy New Jersey. And most of all, enjoy birding!

Good birding,

Jeffrey A Gordon

Jeffrey A. Gordon, *President*
American Birding Association

Birds in New Jersey

The popular imagination sees in New Jersey nothing but airports, highways, and oil refineries, an industrial wasteland punctuated with overpriced suburbs and grimy, overcrowded cities. Birders, on the other hand, see birds.

Happy accidents of geography and a historically strong political will to conservation have made and kept New Jersey one of the finest birding destinations in the world. As a long, tapering peninsula, bounded by river, bay, and open ocean and ribbed by low mountains, New Jersey concentrates migrating birds spring and fall; at all seasons, the state's remarkable range of habitats welcomes species typical of the north, the south, the east, and even the west of the continent. In spite of a very long, not always well-considered history of human development, many of those habitats are still preserved in zealously protected refuges created by local, state, and national authorities.

As a result, some 460 species of birds have been observed in New Jersey since the 17th century. Of those, approximately 375 are recorded in any given year by the combined efforts of the state's hundreds of active birders; the record for a single observer in a single year is (as of 2013) an impressive 362.

Present from March to November, the pale Piping Plover breeds on New Jersey's ocean beaches.

Birds in this Guide

This identification guide covers 255 species of annual and more or less common occurrence in New Jersey. The 200 or so species not treated in full are included in the appendix's complete list of New Jersey birds (as of 2013); among them are oceanic species only very infrequently seen from land, nocturnal birds seldom encountered without a specific search, and a large number of very local species and genuine rarities (known as "accidentals") recorded only a few times or at great intervals over the years.

The 255 species included in this guide are arranged — with a few minor departures to make comparison easier — in the sequence propounded in the *Check-list of the American Ornithologists' Union,* as updated in annual supplements through 2013. New birders (and even many veterans) will find this arrangement anything but intuitive, but it is worth learning, as it reflects the latest scientific views on the relationships and evolutionary history of our birds.

Thus, the most ancient groups are treated at the beginning of the book, with the most recently arisen groups at the end. There are a couple of easy tricks, rules of thumb, to help birders learn the rough sequence of birds and to keep them from wasting time flipping through the pages or poring over an index or table of contents:

- ► Large birds generally come before small birds.

- ► Water birds generally come before land birds.

- ► Simply patterned birds generally come before intricately marked or more colorful birds.

Each of these rules has its exceptions, naturally, but the birder who keeps them in mind will have no trouble remembering that swans — huge, monotone water birds — are described early on in a field guide, while orioles — rather small, brightly colored birds of the treetops — should be sought towards its end.

Many birders find it helpful to memorize the placement of a few groups to serve as landmarks. Knowing that geese are first, sparrows and finches last, and falcons and parrots in the very middle of the guide can make it easier to "triangulate" the position of other groups.

How to Use the Species Accounts

Each of the species accounts begins with the official English and scientific names of the bird; these, too, are determined by the AOU *Check-list*. The English names of birds are capitalized here to make them easier to pick out in the text.

The scientific names comprise a capitalized genus name and a lower-case species name; the genus name indicates presumed evolutionary relationship: thus, *Passerina caerulea* and *Passerina cyanea* can be seen to be closely related and in some ways similar—a fact often not apparent in the English names, in this case, Blue Grosbeak and Indigo Bunting.

The measurements that follow are those of an average bird. Size, especially length, can be difficult to judge in the field, and it is always helpful to compare an unknown bird with another, familiar species or even with the twig or post it might be perched on; bird feeders can provide an excellent yardstick to gauge the length of the birds visiting them.

Mass (or "weight") is usually more eloquent than length. A Great Cormorant, for example, is only about 4 inches longer than the similar Double-crested Cormorant, but it outweighs its smaller cousin by 90 percent (7.3 vs. 3.7 pounds); with a little experience, that difference can often be obvious even at a distance.

The text accounts usually begin with a general impression of the bird's size and shape. Such terms as large and small, or slender and bulky, should be understood as comparisons to similar, closely related species: obviously, even a very large sparrow will be significantly smaller than even the smallest goose.

Shape in most birds is determined by the size and structure of the tail, wings, head, and bill, and those features are emphasized in the text's descriptions. Again, a tail (or bill or head or wing) described as long will be long in comparison to that of a similar species. Making such judgments may seem difficult at first, but keeping them in mind while reviewing the photographs and, best of all, while watching birds in the field can train the eye to recognize even very small differences.

Most of the birds treated in this guide are common
or even abundant species, but some are uncommon (reliably
present in the appropriate season but not reliably found)
or scarce (usually present in the appropriate season but in
such low numbers as not to be expected on any given excursion).
A few truly rare birds—present, often only irregularly,
in very small numbers—are sufficiently large, conspicuous,
or colorful to merit inclusion; the most obvious example
is the Harlequin Duck, no more than a few dozen of which are
ever found in New Jersey.

The weirdly beautiful
Harlequin Duck is rare,
but conspicuous around
wintertime jetties.

Abundant in New
Jersey woodlands, the
cryptically colored
American Woodcock is
rarely noticed.

Bird Habitats

Even the most common species are found only in particular
habitats. Some associations are very strict: Common Eider
are not found in mountaintop forests, and White-breasted
Nuthatches should not be expected on wide-open sandy
beaches. Other species are more opportunistic in the range of
habitats they use, and in the case of long-distance migrants,
most bets are off in spring and fall, when birds of the deepest
woodland or of the ocean vastness can appear anywhere.

New Jersey's most important habitats and some of their
characteristic birds include:

HABITAT	BIRDS
Open ocean and Delaware Bay	Scoters, Northern Gannet, Red-throated Loon
Jetties and breakwaters	Common Eider, Dunlin, Purple Sandpiper
Back bays	Long-tailed Duck, herons, Laughing Gull
Ocean and barrier beaches	American Oystercatcher, Sanderling, Snow Bunting
Salt marshes	American Black Duck, Willet, Seaside Sparrow
Rivers	Common Merganser, Green Heron, Bald Eagle
Lakes and reservoirs	Snow Goose, gulls, Belted Kingfisher
Freshwater marshes	Virginia Rail, Common Yellowthroat, Swamp Sparrow
Grasslands	Ring-necked Pheasant, Grasshopper Sparrow, Eastern Meadowlark
Farmland	Wild Turkey, Red-tailed Hawk
Old fields	Prairie Warbler, Blue Grosbeak, Field Sparrow
Deciduous forests	Yellow-bellied Sapsucker, Wood Thrush, Winter Wren
Pine barrens	Red-bellied Woodpecker, Pine Warbler, Eastern Towhee
Suburbs	Eastern Screech-Owl, Northern Mockingbird, Dark-eyed Junco
Cities	Gulls, Rock Pigeon, House Sparrow
Corporate parks	Canada Goose

Common Mergansers, as their name implies, are common winter visitors to New Jersey's lakes and reservoirs.

Some very common birds can be found wherever the appropriate habitat persists. For many others, less common or more locally distributed, the text offers a few suggestions for sites where a given species might be more easily seen. Wherever possible in such cases, we have recommended well-known and frequently visited birding destinations that are likely to produce not just the "target species" but a wide range of sightings besides; as a result, places such as Sandy Hook, Brigantine NWR, and Cape May are mentioned repeatedly for species that could also be found at other, less generally productive sites.

Bird Sounds

The text for most species ends with a short description of the bird's calls and songs, often with a transcription of the most distinctive notes or phrases. Given the abundance of free and readily accessible recordings of bird vocalizations on the internet, these descriptions and transliterations are not necessarily intended to teach the new birder these specific songs; instead, they are meant as examples of the types of descriptive terms and mnemonic techniques that can make a sound learned in the field or from a recording more memorable. The best "ear birders" eventually develop their own, often idiosyncratic vocabularies for describing what they hear, and new birders should take the descriptions offered here as inspiration to elaborate their own individual terminologies.

The musical caroling song of the Common Yellowthroat is part of the spring soundscape of salt and freshwater marshes.

The Parts of Birds

Each of the 255 species treated in the main text is illustrated
by one to three photographs, many of them taken in New
Jersey and all of them showing birds from the same geographic
populations that breed, winter, or migrate through the state.
Where the ages and sexes of a species differ visually, the
first illustration usually depicts the least colorful or least
distinctive age or sex class, and the caption focuses first on
characteristics of size, shape, or habit shared by both sexes and
all ages. The captions to the other illustration or illustrations
point out the specific marks distinguishing females from males
and adults from young birds. Read together, the photograph
captions and the prose text should provide all the information
needed to identify the bird in all age and sex classes and to
find it in the correct season and habitat.

Though technical terms have been avoided as much as
possible in both the main entries and captions, some specialized
language is needed to describe the parts of birds economically.

Knowing these basic terms will help the user of this guide
concentrate on the parts of the bird most relevant to identification. In addition to size and shape, the markings of wings, tail,
and head are usually the most important.

PARTS OF A DUCK
This male Blue-winged Teal shows the important visible parts of a duck on the water's surface.

crown

wing tip

back

nape

forehead

breast

tail

"fender"

flank

side

neck

undertail

PARTS OF A GULL
This adult Ring-billed Gull shares many aspects with other gulls.

crown

forehead

nape

throat

back

neck

breast

belly

foot

wing tip

tail

toes

PARTS OF A RAPTOR
This perched Cooper's Hawk shows the features shared by many raptors.

crown

back

nape

forehead

secondaries

primaries

tail

throat

neck

breast

belly

vent

flank

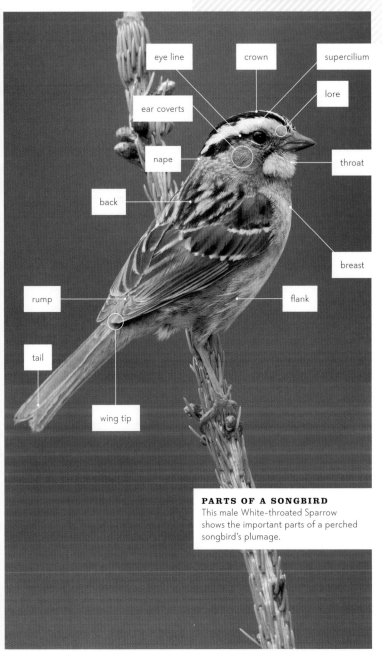

eye line

crown

supercilium

lore

ear coverts

nape

throat

back

breast

rump

flank

tail

wing tip

PARTS OF A SONGBIRD
This male White-throated Sparrow
shows the important parts of a perched
songbird's plumage.

FLIGHT FEATHERS The long "quills" of wing and tail. The flight feathers of the wing are divided into secondaries (on the inner part of the wing, closer to the body) and primaries (on the outer part of the wing, away from the body).

The slaty flight feathers of a Tricolored Heron are sharply set off from the white belly and underwing.

WING BAR A contrasting pale line (often paired), vertical on the folded wing.

The wingbars of a White-winged Crossbill are wide and bright white.

Both crossbill species are irregularly common winter visitors to New Jersey, where they feed in conifers and sweetgums, using their distinctive bills to pry seeds loose. Red Crossbills often have weak brown or whitish wingbars.

WING STRIPE A contrasting pale band across the flight feathers, often concealed on the folded wing.

Barely hinted at in the perched bird, the wing stripe of a Willet is startling in flight.

TAIL BAND
A contrasting bar across the tip of the tail.

The Magnolia Warbler's white tail with a broad black tail band is unlike that of any other songbird.

TAIL EDGE
A contrasting band along the sides of the tail.

Light, distance, and the observer's angle can make the usually low-contrast tail edges of an American Tree Sparrow more conspicuous.

UNDERTAIL The wedge of short feathers at the base of the tail on the underside of the bird. Moving forward on the underparts, the next areas are the vent (between the legs), the belly, the breast, and the throat; the flanks, largely concealed on the perched bird by the wing, border the belly and breast.

Even the brownest Palm Warbler shows a distinctive bright yellow undertail.

HEAD The top of the head, the crown, is sometimes bordered by stripes. Some birds have a supercilium (above the eye) or an eye line (through the eye). The triangular patch beneath and behind the eye is the ear coverts. Many birds show a pale eye ring.

Male Ruby-crowned Kinglets can conceal—and reveal—their bright crown patches at will.

SUPERCILIUM
A contrasting line above the eye.

EYE LINE
A contrasting line through the eye.

Dull Eastern Meadowlarks in fall still show a distinctive blackish eye line and broad white supercilium contrasting with pale, gray-streaked ear coverts.

WING TIP   The end of the spread wing farthest from the body. On a perched bird, the wing tip is furled just above the tail; its length can be measured by how far it protrudes from the rest of the folded wing or by how far it extends in relation to the tail.

The Eastern Bluebird's off-white belly, vent, and undertail are set off by the rusty orange of the flank, breast, and throat.

At a distance, the bright white throat of a Swamp Sparrow is more visible than any other plumage character.

RUMP   The square of sometimes contrasting feathers on the upperparts, just above the base of the tail. Moving forward on the upperparts, the next areas are the back and the nape (rear of the head).

This winter male American Goldfinch's wingtip almost covers the bird's pale yellow and white rump.

All Hairy Woodpeckers show a long white back patch, but only males have a red spot on the nape.

Identifying Birds

The organization of the main entries and captions is meant to encourage a specific approach to identifying an unfamiliar bird. Habitat, season, and relative abundance will allow the observer to eliminate many possibilities from the very start. While a few birds may be instantly identifiable by color or pattern, in the great majority of cases it is best to begin with a consideration of size and shape. Assessing the shape of the bill, whether fine or thick, straight or curved, is useful, but when faced with an unknown bird, it is always most helpful (even if perhaps slightly counter-intuitive) to start not at the front of the bird but at the rear, for a sense of the bird's wing and tail. They are, after all, the physical structures most obviously involved in the most distinctive behavior of North America's birds—flight—and their length and shape are often enough all by themselves to distinguish species that may otherwise be very similar in plumage and pattern.

As the observer's eye moves forward, the color, length, and thickness of the feet and legs are the next features to note. The fullness of breast and belly and the shape of the back, flat or arched, also sometimes differ between closely related species. Finally, the head pattern is worth looking closely at in many birds. In the predominantly small songbirds where it truly matters, the markings of the head—lateral crown stripes, supercilia, eye lines, eye rings, and other subtle characters—are often so fine as to be practically invisible in themselves, but they often contribute to a distinctive "facial expression." A pale eye ring, for example, can create an open, "innocent" aspect, while a dark eye line may create an impression of "fierceness" or "sternness." Here too, as in learning and remembering vocalizations, it can help to develop a personal vocabulary for describing such impressions in an easily memorable way.

Birding Sites in New Jersey

New Jersey birders are fortunate to have one of the finest
site guides ever written, William Boyle's *Guide to Bird
Finding in New Jersey*, with entries covering more than 130
places throughout the state. Boyle's book should always
be consulted for directions and full birding information. The
localities recommended in this guide include the following
sites, listed alphabetically.

SITE	COUNTY	SEASON	BIRDS
Alpha	Warren	Winter, summer	Breeding and wintering land birds, hawks
Assunpink WMA	Monmouth	Fall, winter, spring	Water birds, grassland birds, migrant landbirds
Avalon	Cape May	Fall, winter	Seabirds
Barnegat Light	Ocean	Winter	Waterfowl, seabirds, gulls
Belleplain State Forest	Cape May	Spring and summer	Migrant and nesting land birds
Brigantine NWR	Atlantic	All seasons	Water and marsh birds
Bull's Island State Park	Hunterdon	Spring and summer	Migrant and nesting land birds
Byrne State Forest	Burlington	Spring	Migrant and nesting land birds
Cape May	Cape May	All seasons	All birds, all the time
Chimney Rock	Somerset	Fall	Migrant hawks
Cold Brook Reserve	Hunterdon	Fall	Migrant land birds
DeKorte Park	Bergen	All seasons	Water and marsh birds, migrant land birds
Dividing Creek	Cumberland	All seasons	Water and marsh birds, raptors, migrant and nesting land birds
Duke Farms	Somerset	Spring and summer	Nesting grassland birds
Fort Lee Historic Park	Bergen	Spring	Raptors, migrant land birds

SITE	COUNTY	SEASON	BIRDS
Garret Mountain	Passaic	Fall, winter, spring	Migrant and wintering land birds
Glassboro Woods	Gloucester	Spring and summer	Migrant and nesting land birds
Glenhurst Meadows	Somerset	Summer and fall	Migrant and nesting land birds, field birds
Great Swamp NWR	Somerset/Morris	All seasons	Water and marsh birds, migrant land birds
Heislerville	Cumberland	Summer, fall	Shorebirds
High Point State Park	Sussex	Spring, summer	Migrant and nesting land birds
Island Beach State Park	Ocean	All seasons	Water, marsh, and sea birds; migrant and nesting land birds
Jakes Landing	Cape May	All seasons	Marsh birds, raptors, nesting and migrant land birds
Kearny Marsh	Bergen	All seasons	Marsh birds
Liberty Sod Farm	Warren	Fall	Migrant shorebirds
Liberty State Park	Hudson	Fall, winter, spring	Water and marsh birds, migrant and wintering land birds
Manahawkin	Ocean	Winter	Marsh birds, raptors
Manasquan Inlet	Monmouth/ Ocean	Winter	Seabirds
Mannington Marsh	Salem	Spring and summer	Water and marsh birds
Meadowlands	Bergen	All seasons	Water and marsh birds
Mercer County Lake	Mercer	Fall, winter, spring	Water and marsh birds, migrant land birds
Merrill Creek Reservoir	Warren	Fall and winter	Raptors and waterfowl
Mills Reservation	Essex	Fall and spring	Raptors, migrant land birds
Montclair Hawk Watch	Essex	Fall and spring	Migrant raptors
Negri-Nepote Preserve	Somerset	Spring and summer	Nesting grassland birds

SITE	COUNTY	SEASON	BIRDS
New Jersey Brigade Area	Somerset	Spring and summer	Migrant and nesting land birds
North Shore Ponds	Monmouth	Winter	Waterfowl and seabirds
Nummy Island	Cape May	All seasons	Water and marsh birds
Oradell Reservoir	Bergen	Fall	Waterfowl
Palmyra Cove	Burlington	Fall	Migrant land birds
Pedricktown Marshes	Salem	Spring	Waterfowl, shorebirds
Rogers Refuge	Mercer	Spring, summer, fall	Water and marsh birds, migrant and nesting land birds
Raritan Bay	Middlesex/ Monmouth	Winter and spring	Waterfowl, seabirds
Rifle Camp Park	Passaic	Spring	Raptors, migrant land birds
Round Valley Reservoir	Hunterdon	Winter	Waterfowl, gulls
Sandy Hook	Monmouth	All seasons	Water, marsh, and seabirds; raptors; migrant land birds
Scherman Hoffman Sanctuary	Somerset	Spring and summer	Migrant and nesting land birds
Shark River	Monmouth	Winter	Waterfowl, seabirds
Six Mile Run	Somerset	Spring and summer	Migrant and nesting field birds
Spruce Run Reservoir	Hunterdon	Fall, winter	Waterfowl, owls, wintering land birds
Stokes State Forest	Sussex	Spring, summer	Nesting landbirds, hawks
Stone Harbor	Cape May	All seasons	Water and sea birds, nesting terns and skimmers
Trenton-Hamilton Marsh	Mercer	All seasons	Marsh birds
Troy Meadows	Morris	All seasons	Marsh birds, raptors, migrant land birds

SITE	COUNTY	SEASON	BIRDS
Tuckerton	Ocean	All seasons	Water and marsh birds, migrant and nesting land birds
Vernon Crossing Marsh	Sussex	Spring	Migrant and nesting marsh and land birds
Walker Avenue Wetlands	Passaic	Spring and fall	Water and marsh birds, migrant land birds
Walkill NWR	Sussex	All seasons	Raptors, owls, migrant and nesting land birds
Worthington State Forest	Warren	Spring and summer	Migrant and nesting land birds

A Year Afield

The two dozen excursions suggested here take the birder through a full year and a wide range of New Jersey habitats.

MONTH		
August	Stone Harbor	Walker Avenue Wetlands
September	Cape May	Palmyra
October	Montclair Hawk Watch	Cold Brook Reserve
November	Brigantine NWR	Island Beach
December	Liberty State Park	Jakes Landing
January	North Shore Ponds	Manahawkin
February	Barnegat Light	Alpha
March	Spruce Run	Pedricktown
April	Belleplain	Tuckerton
May	Garret Mountain	Duke Farms
June	Negri-Nepote	High Point
July	Worthington	Sandy Hook

Additional Resources

The authoritative source on the status and distribution of New Jersey birds is William Boyle's *Birds of New Jersey* (Princeton UP, 2011). Detailed maps for all of the state's breeding species as of 1997 were published in Joan Walsh et al.'s *Birds of New Jersey* (NJ Audubon, 1999). Up-to-the-minute observations are available on line at eBird.org, a free database created and maintained by the Cornell Lab of Ornithology; rarities are evaluated and discussed at njbrc.net.

Boyle's *Guide to Bird Finding in New Jersey* (Rutgers UP, 2002) is an indispensable tool for the traveling birder. New sites are regularly described on line at ebird.org/nj.

This guide permits the identification of most of the birds most frequently observed in New Jersey. The state's remaining 200 species are covered in the standard field guides to the birds of North America north of Mexico. The very detailed accounts in Jon Dunn and Jonathan Alderfer's *National Geographic Field Guide to the Birds of North America* (National Geographic, 2011) cover all of the species recorded from the area. David Sibley's *The Sibley Guide to Birds* (Knopf, 2014) is just as richly informative. Either title is very highly recommended as the basic guide for any birder interested in learning more.

American Birding Association

Field Guide to Birds
of New Jersey

Canada Goose

Branta canadensis

L 45″ | **WS** 60″ | **WT** 9.8 LB (4,500 G) | ♂ > ♀

This is the familiar gray-brown, black-necked goose of parks, ponds, playing fields, and corporate lawns. Very large, long-necked, long-billed birds were introduced to New Jersey in the mid-twentieth century, and can now be seen year-round in all but densely wooded habitats; migrants from northerly populations, abundant in winter, are smaller and thicker-necked, with shorter bills and more angular heads.

Historically breeding only in the West and North, Canada Geese now nest over most of the continent. Breeding birds are aggressively territorial, chasing other birds and even humans away from the nest and young with noisy wingbeats.

A loud, low-pitched, disyllabic *ca-RUNK* is heard throughout the year.

Medium-brown body and pale breast contrast with black neck and head; white cheek patch varies in size and shape. Bill and feet blackish.

Alert birds very long-necked. Pale breast separates from Brant, oval head and long bill from rare Cackling Goose.

A strong flyer, flocks often in sharply angled Vs. Easily identified by loud, sonorous honking; at close range, black neck conspicuous.

Brant

Branta bernicla

L 25″ | **WS** 42″ | **WT** 3.1 LB (1,400 G) | ♂ > ♀

Highly social and often very tame, the small, stout, dark Brant is a common winter resident of bays and marshes along the entire New Jersey coast. It can sometimes be detected passing high overland in November and March, especially in the northern part of the state; flocks move in irregular lines or clusters. Good looks at the species are nearly guaranteed in cold weather at Sandy Hook, coastal ponds and estuaries between Belmar and Point Pleasant, and Brigantine NWR. Brant breed on the Arctic coasts of Alaska and Canada; non-breeding birds are infrequent in New Jersey during the summer.

Brant feed in flocks of up to several hundred birds on marshes and lawns and in shallow saltwater. An almost exclusive preference for eelgrass caused a crash in numbers in the 1930s, when that plant was nearly wiped out.

Feeding birds are fairly quiet, but in flight flocks of Brant utter a constant low-pitched purring growl.

Dark, saltwater-loving goose with black breast, neck, and head; adults have narrow, neat white band across the upper neck. Often grazes on lawns near bays and ponds.

Cackling Goose
Branta hutchinsii

L 25″ │ **WS** 43″ │ **WT** 3.5 LB (1,600 G) │ ♂ > ♀

Scarce but rapidly increasing in the state, the small, compact Cackling Goose appears in small numbers each winter on lakes and fields anywhere in New Jersey. Careful, patient searching can turn up individuals and apparent family groups in any large flock of Canada Geese from October to March. Feeding birds spend their days on agricultural fields and large, grassy parks, where they can be difficult to pick out among the larger geese; it is sometimes more productive to sort through the flocks roosting on small lakes.

The high-pitched whistling calls of Cackling Geese are distinctive, but are often drowned out by the honking of their larger companions.

Like a miniature, thick-set Canada Goose. Proportionately short, thick neck ends in small, angular head with pronounced forehead. Short, triangular bill with high base. Usually seen with Canada Geese.

Snow Goose

Chen caerulescens

L 28-31 | **WS** 53-56″ | **WT** 5.3-7.5 LB | ♂ > ♀

Cold-season gatherings of this large, noisy white goose at such favored sites as Brigantine NWR and Merrill Creek Reservoir can easily number in the tens of thousands. Common in winter in southern New Jersey's coastal salt marshes, in migration (October–November and February–March) it can also be found in large numbers on the northern reservoirs, and long, undulating lines or clumps can be seen or heard passing overhead anywhere in the state. A rare dark form, the "Blue Goose," with a dusky gray body and white head and neck, can sometimes be found in these flocks.

This species breeds along the coasts of northern Alaska and Canada, but the odd injured or immature bird sometimes summers in our area.

Snow Geese give an incessant loud, high-pitched, metallic, single-noted call; quieter on the ground, flocks can be almost deafening in flight.

Snowy white body with satiny black wingtips, sometimes invisible on perched birds. Large bill swollen at the base, with broad black "lips."

Clear black wingtips contrast with bright white body and long neck in flight.

Bulky, angular shape when perched, with relatively slender neck and large, long head and large bill. Juveniles are mottled dusky, but black wingtips the darkest part of plumage.

Mute Swan

Cygnus olor

L 60″ | **WS** 75″ | **WT** 22 LB (10 KG) | ♂ > ♀

Introduced from Europe, the enormous Mute Swan breeds
and winters across New Jersey, especially in coastal marshes.
Cape May, Brigantine NWR, and the Meadowlands are good
places to see this species.

Intruders, including humans, are often driven away from
the nest with spread wings.

In spite of their name, adult Mute Swans produce grunts
and hisses. The wings make a loud, low-pitched pulsing hum
in flight.

Noticeably long tail, boxcar-shaped
body, and very slender, curved neck;
juveniles sooty brown to pale gray. Flat,
"duck-like" orange bill with black knob.

Tundra Swan
Cygnus columbianus

L 52″ | **WS** 66″ | **WT** 14.4 LB (6,600 G) | ♂ > ♀

This relatively small, short-necked native swan is uncommon in fall and spring and a scarce winter bird in coastal areas. Flocks, of up to several dozen, produce a high-pitched breathy hooting on the water and in the air. Migrants pass over land, but they are most readily observed at Brigantine NWR or on the Delaware Bayshore in November and February.

Short tail, relatively short neck usually held straight. Adults pure white, black bill often with a yellow basal spot of variable size and shape. Juveniles sooty blue-gray, with variable pink on long, wedge-shaped bill.

Wood Duck

Aix sponsa

L 18.5″ | **WS** 30″ | **WT** 1.3 LB (600 G) | ♂ > ♀

The colorful Wood Duck is one of New Jersey's most abundant breeding ducks, nesting wherever swamps and streams are lined with large trees. Present over most of the state from March to October, this species is easily found in spring and summer at Brigantine NWR, Trenton-Hamilton Marsh, Great Swamp NWR, or Assunpink WMA, and can be seen in migration on nearly any body of fresh water in the state.

As its name suggests, this is the most arboreal of our waterfowl, breeding in woodpecker holes and nest boxes 25 feet or more above the ground. Hatchlings are light enough to jump out of the nest without injury, and follow their mother to the nearest wetland.

Sometimes hard to see in the wooded habitats they prefer, Wood Ducks are easily detected by voice. Males give a soft, rising, wiry *oooeeer*, often while perched on a branch; females call a loud, shrieking *wheeUPP* when flushed. Both sexes are generally silent in sustained flight.

Long, square tail; rectangular body; and large crested head identify both sexes. Colorful male with white bar on side of breast and complex face pattern.

Female with softly dappled sides and speckled breast. Gray head, puffy crest, and bright white "teardrop" surrounding eye; chin and base of bill outlined white.

In flight, long, square tail and neatly set-off white belly; wings dark above with white trailing edge. Large head often held above the horizontal.

Mallard

Anas platyrhynchos

L 23″ | **WS** 35″ | **WT** 2.4 LB (1,100 G) | ♂ > ♀

North America's most familiar duck, the large and sturdy Mallard is a common resident across New Jersey, its numbers swelling during migration and in winter, when it can be seen on virtually any body of fresh water.

Breeding birds occur in parks and on lakes and ponds anywhere in the state. Coastally, the Mallard often breeds with American Black Ducks, producing hybrids and backcrosses that look like Black Ducks with green on the head or white in the tail. Another identification pitfall is provided by domestic Mallards, which show a range of plumages from all white to glossy black and are often released or escape to join wild birds.

This species' voice is essentially identical to that of the American Black Duck. The male has a weak, hoarse croak; the female's usual call is a loud, descending series of harsh quacks.

Long body, deep chest, long head and bill. Colorful male with white neck ring; green, blue, or purple head; and bright white tail topped by curled black feathers.

White tail contrasts with female's rich brown, intricately marked body plumage. Blue or purple patch on inner wing broadly edged white. Long, scooped bill variably blotched orange and black.

White tail and blue and white wing patch conspicuous in flight.

American Black Duck

Anas rubripes

L 23" | **WS** 35" | **WT** 2.6 LB (1,200 G) | ♂ > ♀

Historically one of the most abundant ducks in eastern North America, the American Black Duck has still not completely recovered from overhunting in the nineteenth and twentieth centuries. New Jersey's wintering population is nevertheless the largest on the East Coast. Unlike other dabbling ducks, this species displays a marked preference for salt and brackish water, and though frequently seen inland, is most common at coastal sites such as Sandy Hook, Brigantine NWR, and Cape May.

Smaller numbers nest in salt marshes and occasionally on inland ponds. Mixed pairs with Mallards are not unusual; their offspring show a mixture of characteristics.

This species' voice is essentially identical to that of the closely related Mallard. The male has a weak, hoarse croak; the female's usual call is a loud, descending series of harsh quacks.

Dark tail, sooty to blackish body plumage, contrasting buffy-tan neck and head, and green (male) or grayish green bill (female) distinguish this species from Mallard.

Dark body contrasts with paler neck and head and flashing white underwing. Tail and trailing edge of wing without white.

Hybrids with Mallard show varying amounts of white in tail and wing, green on head of males.

Gadwall

Anas strepera

L 20″ | **WS** 33″ | **WT** 2 LB (910 G) | ♂ > ♀

Often overlooked, the discreetly colored Gadwall is a common migrant and wintering bird on bodies of water throughout the state, with much smaller numbers breeding, especially in the Meadowlands. From October through March, these ducks are easily found on coastal ponds from Sandy Hook to Cape May and at inland ponds and lakes; they can be especially abundant in the shallow pools of Brigantine NWR.

Female Gadwalls are fairly quiet, giving an occasional undistinguished Mallard-like quack. Courting males utter an almost constant croaking *vrrp,* quiet but far-carrying, a characteristic background sound of winter ponds.

Square head with full nape and steep forehead. Male's black rear borders gray of flank with no white "fender" between; speckled gray breast and slender, dark bill.

In flight, white belly and plain wing from beneath; above, both sexes show distinctive square white patch on inner wing.

Eurasian Wigeon

Anas mareca

L 20″ | **WS** 32″ | **WT** 1.5 LB (690 G) | ♂ > ♀

A rare but regular visitor from October to March, the chubby, round-headed Eurasian Wigeon makes annual appearances on freshwater lakes and marshes throughout the state. The colorful male is often conspicuous in large wintertime waterfowl flocks, but females are easily overlooked among other brown ducks, especially American Wigeon. Some individuals return to the same wintering site year after year; favored locations over the years have included Cape May, Brigantine NWR, and the shore ponds of Monmouth County, but this species can occur anywhere in New Jersey.

Rounded head appears larger than American Wigeon's. Male's gray body contrasts with rosy breast and deep copper head with creamy forehead; often some green around eye.

Females usually darker and more reddish than American Wigeon, many with distinctive rusty head.

American Wigeon

Anas americana

L 20" | **WS** 32" | **WT** 1.6 LB (720 G) | ♂ > ♀

The round-headed, long-tailed, short-billed American Wigeon is a common wintering bird in marshes and on ponds and lakes throughout the state. Typically a bird of fresh water, it can also be seen on saltwater bays and even the ocean, where it stays close to shore. Wigeons are most abundant and easily seen on the ponds at Brigantine NWR, Cape May, and other coastal sites.

Though wigeons are dabbling ducks, capturing small animals and gathering aquatic vegetation by tipping up in the water, they also spend considerable time grazing on land. They are also insistent pirates, stealing food brought to the surface by diving American Coots.

While females are very quiet, male American Wigeons are among the most vocal of our winter ducks. The most commonly heard call is a series of three loud, slightly breathy, high-pitched whistles *whew-whee-whew*, the central note louder and higher-pitched than the others.

Long, pointed tail; oval body; large round head; and short bill identify both sexes. Male's rusty body contrasts with paler gray head with dark eye stripe and bright white forehead.

Female's pinkish-orange body contrasts with gray head; often darkest around eye. Short bill blue-gray with black tip.

Pointed tail, large head, and white belly distinctive in flight. Square patch on inner forewing bright white in males, duller in females.

Northern Pintail

Anas acuta

L 21″ | **WS** 34″ | **WT** 1.8LB (800 G) | ♂ > ♀

Very gregarious, with flocks regularly numbering in the thousands, the handsome, long-necked and long-tailed Northern Pintail is a common migrant and winter resident on most of the larger bodies of water in New Jersey, especially near the coast. This species is an early migrant in both spring and fall, often arriving by late August and departing in huge flocks by early March. Thousands can be seen in late winter at Brigantine NWR, the northern reservoirs, and the Pedricktown marshes.

Like other dabbling ducks, pintails feed by tipping up; their long necks let them feed in deeper water than most of their relatives.

Northern Pintails are relatively quiet much of the year. In late winter, small parties of males pursue females through the air, giving a series of loud, somewhat quavering whistles with little variation in pitch.

Long, flat body with long, pointed tail and long, slender neck. Male with very long central tail feathers, silvery body with white neck and breast and chocolate head.

Female cold brown, with long, pointed tail and long neck. Dark eye stands out on faintly marked tan head, which contrasts with dark, slender bill.

Tail, neck, and wings all long and pointed. Head often held slightly below level of body in flight.

Blue-winged Teal

Anas discors

L 15.5″ | **WS** 23″ | **WT** 13 OZ (380 G) | ♂ > ♀

This small, slender duck is a common migrant and scarce summer resident statewide. Unlike most waterfowl, the Blue-winged Teal is extremely cold-sensitive, and this is one of New Jersey's rarest ducks in winter. Peak migration periods are April and August–September, when this species can be found on ponds and lakes anywhere in the state. Great Swamp, Brigantine NWR, and Cape May are all reliable sites.

As in most ducks, the colorful breeding plumage is worn only in winter and spring. In the breeding season, both sexes molt into a duller, brown plumage, and the otherwise bright males resemble the females.

Blue-winged Teal are quiet much of the year, but courting males in late winter and spring give a long series of high-pitched, chirping whistles, resembling the peeping of baby chicks.

Slender body, small head, long bill. Male with white "fender" patch and large white crescent contrasting with blue-gray head.

Female evenly gray-brown, with flank and undertail paler. Pale head with broken eye line, vague white spot at base of contrasting dark bill.

Uniform underparts and powder-blue wing patch conspicuous in flight.

Northern Shoveler

Anas clypeata

L 19" | **WS** 30" | **WT** 1.3 LB (610 G) | ♂ > ♀

Flocks of this rather small, distinctively long-billed duck often form "pinwheels" on the water of ponds and coastal impoundments, swimming in tight circles to bring food to the surface. The Northern Shoveler is a common migrant and winter resident in New Jersey, arriving as early as August and most departing by April. The Meadowlands, Brigantine NWR, and the North Shore ponds are good locations to see large numbers of Northern Shovelers at close range.

Northern Shovelers are not especially vocal; a low, hoarse muttering is sometimes heard from feeding flocks. On flushing, the wings make a crashing sound louder than the wingbeats of other dabbling ducks.

Long neck, head, and bill; powder-blue wing patch conspicuous in flight.

Except for spectacular bill and pale powder-blue wing patch, female resembles female Mallard: mottled brown, with contrasting white tail.

Long, shoebox-shaped body with large head and very long, flare-tipped bill. Male with white breast setting off bright rusty flanks and dark, green- or blue-glossed head.

Green-winged Teal

Anas crecca

L 14″ | **WS** 23″ | **WT** 12 OZ (350 G) | ♂ > ♀

The chubby, square-headed Green-winged Teal is an abundant migrant and a common winter resident of muddy ponds, lakes, and marshes. These very small ducks prefer to feed in shallow water or even on mudflats, where they push themselves through the muck on their breasts and bellies.

While this species can appear on any body of fresh water, some of the largest concentrations can be seen in October at Brigantine NWR and in March at the Pedricktown marshes. The earliest autumn birds arrive by September, and most leave the state in April.

The breathy, insistently repeated cricket-like whistle of courting male Green-winged Teal is a characteristic background noise in winter wetlands.

Stubby body with large, square head and short bill. Male with gray body, creamy rear end, vertical white breast stripe, and rusty head with dark green eye patch.

Female richly barred and speckled brown, with creamy patch beneath tail. Strong dark eye line and small pale spot at base of dark bill.

Short neck makes head look large in flight. Well-defined oval white belly, narrow whitish stripe across underwing.

Canvasback
Aythya valisineria

L 21″ | **WS** 29″ | **WT** 2.7 LB (1,220 G) | ♂ > ♀

The largest of the black-breasted diving ducks, the low-floating, slope-headed Canvasback is an uncommon migrant and winter visitor on bays and freshwater lakes and ponds. This is a cold-weather species in New Jersey, not usually arriving until November and departing in March. Flocks numbering into the low hundreds can usually be found at DeKorte Park or Brigantine NWR, with smaller numbers on inland reservoirs and the North Shore ponds.

Canvasbacks are quiet in the winter.

Long, low-slung body with thick neck and long, oval head sloping into evenly tapered black bill. Male with dull white body, small black breast patch, dark rusty head.

Female with pale gray body, small dark breast patch, evenly tapered dark bill.

Redhead

Aythya americana

L 19″ | **WS** 29″ | **WT** 2.3 LB (1,050 G) | ♂ > ♀

Somber-colored, compact, and round-headed, Redheads are scarce and probably declining winter visitors to inland waters and coastal ponds and bays in New Jersey, arriving in November and departing by early April. Single birds or, more rarely, small flocks of this typically western duck can be encountered on the North Shore ponds and the northern reservoirs, where they are often found feeding in the company of American Coots and American Wigeons.

Short body with high back and rounded head; forehead descends steeply to short, colorful bill. Male with dark gray body, extensive black breast, red head, black-tipped blue bill.

Female uniformly dull brown, head usually with white eye ring and diffuse white patch at base of bicolored bill. In flight, both sexes show broad silvery wing stripe.

Greater Scaup
Aythya marila

L 18″ | **WS** 28″ | **WT** 2.3 LB (1,050 G) | ♂ > ♀

The starkly bicolored Greater Scaup is a common winter resident on coastal bays and the ocean; migrants can also be encountered on large bodies of fresh water inland. They arrive in New Jersey in October and depart in April. Greater Scaup can be seen at most coastal birding sites from Sandy Hook to Cape May; large wintering flocks, numbering into the thousands, are often present on Raritan Bay and the Navesink River.

Short body with short tail, high back, and rather small head with full, rounded nape and curved forehead. Wide blue bill has black covering most of tip. Male with white sides and faintly barred white back; rear and extensive breast patch black. Head may show green gloss.

Female dark brown with large, well-defined white patch at base of blue-gray bill. Some females show white comma over ear. In flight, both sexes show white wing stripe nearly reaching wing tip.

Lesser Scaup

Aythya affinis

L 16.5″ | **WS** 25″ | **WT** 1.8 LB (830 G) | ♂ > ♀

A near twin to the slightly larger Greater Scaup, this species is a fairly common migrant on coastal bays and freshwater ponds and lakes; smaller numbers occur in winter. On salt water, large flocks of Greater Scaup often contain a few Lessers, but this species is most common in freshwater habitats. Reliable sites include the northern reservoirs and the North Shore ponds.

Short body with short tail, high back, and rather small head with steep nape and forehead and slightly crested rear crown. Narrow blue bill has black restricted to center of tip. Male with white sides and coarsely barred white back; rear and extensive breast patch black. Head may show purple or green gloss.

Female dark brown with large, well-defined white patch at base of blue-gray bill. In flight, both sexes show white wing stripe restricted to inner wing.

Ring-necked Duck

Aythya collaris

L 17" | **WS** 25" | **WT** 1.5 LB (700 G) | ♂ > ♀

Of the black-breasted diving ducks, the neatly marked, pointy-headed Ring-necked Duck is the species with the greatest fondness for fresh water, and it is rarely seen on bays or the ocean. This is a common and probably increasing migrant and winter visitor on ponds and lakes in New Jersey, arriving in October and departing in April. It is easy to find on the North Shore ponds, the northern reservoirs, and small wooded ponds throughout the state.

Unlike most other diving ducks, Ring-necked Ducks tend to avoid the exposed center of bodies of water, preferring instead to feed near the shore or at the edge of islands.

Short body with long tail, high back, and large, high-peaked head with vertical nape and curved forehead. Male with black back, silvery sides separated from extensive black breast by white wedge. Purple-glossed head; bill with gray saddle and black tip.

Female brown with darker back, head usually with white eye ring and variably well-defined white patch at base of tricolored bill. In flight, both sexes uniformly dark above, with dark gray wing stripe.

Common Eider

Somateria mollissima

L 24″ | **WS** 38″ | **WT** 4.7 LB (2,150 G) | ♂ > ♀

Once very rare in New Jersey, this very large, bulky, bull-nosed sea duck is now a locally common winter resident in turbulent shallow waters off coastal jetties. Migrants can be seen in November and December at Avalon and other coastal outlooks, but the most reliable sites for wintering groups are Sandy Hook, Cape May, and, especially, Barnegat Light, where recent winters have seen a resident flock of more than 100 birds.

Common Eiders are strong divers, plucking mussels and other marine invertebrates from the rocks with their heavy, wedge-shaped bills.

Female Common Eiders tend to be quiet, but courting males in late winter utter an almost constant low-pitched, breathy moan.

Adult male strikingly white-backed and -breasted, with black underparts. Large, blocky head and dull green bill, which meets black cap high on forehead.

Female and young birds gray-brown to chocolate, with conspicuous black barring on sides and long, sloping dark bill.

Harlequin Duck
Histrionicus histrionicus

L 16.5″ | **WS** 26″ | **WT** 1.3 LB (600 G) | ♂ > ♀

The small, long-tailed, and stubby-billed Harlequin Duck is a very local winter resident in turbulent shallow waters off coastal jetties. Migrants are occasionally seen from Avalon and other coastal watch sites, but the only dependable flock in the state is the regular and very tame wintering birds at Barnegat Light, which number twenty or more in most years from November to March. Harlequin Ducks rarely stray more than a few yards from the rocks, and often allow a very close approach.

This species' call is a soft, high-pitched, rising whistled squeal, somewhat similar to the call of a male Wood Duck.

Small, dark, pudgy duck with long tail, large head, and tiny bill. Adult male with distinctive pattern of white bars and spots; bright colors visible at close range.

Female dark cocoa-brown, with small white spot on ear and two diffuse patches on face. Both sexes very dark in flight.

Black Scoter

Melanitta americana

L 19″ | **WS** 28″ | **WT** 2.1 LB (950 G) | ♂ > ♀

This medium-sized, long-tailed, round-headed sea duck is the most abundant of the scoters at most locations in coastal New Jersey during fall migration; many thousands stream south past Avalon in October, when small numbers also stop over on large bodies of fresh water. Wintering birds are most reliably found at Sandy Hook, Barnegat Light, and Cape May.

This is the most vocal of the scoters, males giving a loud, clear, slightly descending whistle in the winter.

Most "duck-like" of the scoters, with long tail often held up, round head, and short bill. Adult male (left) with evenly sooty plumage, orange "butterball" at base of dark bill.

Female blackish, with contrasting black cap and paler cheek. No white on wing in either sex, but underwing can look silvery in flight.

Surf Scoter

Melanitta perspicillata

L 20″ | **WS** 30″ | **WT** 2.1 LB (950 G) | ♂ > ♀

Thousands of this large, slope-headed sea duck fly past Avalon and other coastal sites each October; wintering birds are common at Sandy Hook, Barnegat Light, Cape May, and many places on the New Jersey shore. Small numbers of migrants occasionally stop over on large bodies of fresh water.

In the winter, Surf Scoters commonly flock with eiders, Long-tailed Ducks, and other scoter species; they are often the most common species in such gatherings.

Large, heavy duck with fairly long tail and huge, "stuck-on" triangular bill. Adult male with white on nape and forehead and multi-colored bill.

Female brownish-black, with contrasting black cap and two poorly defined whitish spots on face. No white on wing in either sex.

White-winged Scoter

Melanitta fusca

L 21″ **WS** 34″ | **WT** 3.7 LB (1,670 G) | ♂ > ♀

Once the most abundant of our three scoter species, this large, blocky-headed sea duck is now an uncommon migrant and winter resident on the coast, with small numbers seen inland in migration. The reduction in numbers coastally corresponds with an increase in wintering populations on the Great Lakes. Southbound migrants can be seen reliably at Avalon. Wintering birds occur at Sandy Hook, Barnegat Light, and Cape May.

Long, low-slung body, with long, sloping head and bill. White on wings can be concealed. Adult male with "winking" eye patch, black and yellowish bill.

Female blackish, two defined white spots on face. White on wings, conspicuous in flight, can be concealed in swimming birds.

Long-tailed Duck
Clangula hyemalis

L 16.5″ (ADULT ♂ TO 21″) | **WS** 28″ | **WT** 1.6 LB (740 G) | ♂ > ♀

Small, noisy, and oddly shaped, the Long-tailed Duck is a common migrant and winter resident on large bays and open ocean; especially in late winter, small numbers also occur on lakes inland. Large numbers pass Avalon in November, and wintering birds can be seen at Sandy Hook, Barnegat Bay, and Barnegat Light.

The male Long-tailed Duck is the most vocal of the sea ducks, calling ceaselessly on even the coldest days. The call comprises three loud, breathy whistles, the last slightly metallic and rapidly ascending: *oh, ool, olwhap!*

Stubby body with long tail, long thin neck, and large, angular head. Winter male with very long, pointed tail; largely white plumage sets off dark wings and face, black and pink bill.

Female brown and white, with white face. In flight, no white on wing in either sex.

Common Goldeneye

Bucephala clangula

L 18.5" | **WS** 26" | **WT** 1.9 LB (850 G) | ♂ > ♀

This starkly white, triangular-headed diving duck is an uncommon migrant inland and a fairly common winter resident on the coast and northern reservoirs. A decidedly cold-weather species, most birds arrive in November and depart by late March. While goldeneyes can be found on nearly any body of unfrozen water, Raritan Bay, Sandy Hook, and Barnegat Bay are excellent places to look.

Courting male Common Goldeneyes accompany their head-tossing displays with a dry, high-pitched buzz, a characteristic sound of bays and large lakes in late winter.

Short, high-backed body with outsized head. Steep nape, bulbous crown, and long forehead sloping into short, wedge-shaped bill. Adult male bright white; round white spot at base of bill.

Female silvery gray with coppery head and white throat. White wing patches in both sexes; wingbeats produce a high, bell-like ringing or whistle.

Bufflehead

Bucephala albeola

L 13.5″ │ **WS** 21″ │ **WT** 13 OZ (380 G) │ ♂ > ♀

The tiny, puffy-crowned Bufflehead is a very common migrant and winter resident on both salt water and fresh throughout New Jersey. This smallest of the diving ducks arrives in October and departs again in April. Unlike other diving ducks, it is not particularly gregarious, and Buffleheads tend to scatter over their preferred lakes and bays rather than gather into tight flocks. This species is easily observed on the northern reservoirs and the North Shore ponds, and can be especially common in winter at Sandy Hook, Brigantine NWR, and Cape May.

Small and fat; neckless appearance with large, puffy head and small, triangular bill. Male extensively white with black back and head with large white patch.

Female cold gray-brown with oval white ear patch. In rapid, buzzing flight, white wing patches in both sexes.

Hooded Merganser
Lophodytes cucullatus

L 18″ | **WS** 24″ | **WT** 1.4 LB (620 G) | ♂ > ♀

Common and increasing as a migrant and winter resident, the small, dark, long-tailed Hooded Merganser can be found on fresh water and estuaries throughout the state; a few breed at scattered locations, especially in the north, where they use old woodpecker cavities or nest boxes. Hooded Mergansers are easily found in winter at Brigantine NWR, Cape May, and the North Shore ponds.

Courting males may give a soft buzzy rattle, but both sexes of this species tend to be quiet.

Long tail and long, low-backed body. Head with puffy, fan-shaped crest; narrow, short bill. Adult male dark with white breast and neatly outlined crest.

Female cold gray-brown with reddish-fawn crest; bill dark above, yellow below. In very fast flight, both sexes show small, square white wing patches.

Common Merganser

Mergus merganser

L 25″ | **WS** 34″ | **WT** 3.4 LB (1,530 G) | ♂ > ♀

Fonder of fresh water than are its relatives, this heavy, long-bodied, large-headed duck is a common migrant and winter resident on lakes in the northern two-thirds of the state; small numbers breed on the Delaware River south to Mercer County. Good places to see this species in winter and early spring include Mercer County Lake, Merrill Creek, Spruce Run, and Oradell Reservoir. Families with ducklings can be seen in Worthington State Forest in May and June.

Common Mergansers are among the most silent of our ducks, but may give a soft croaking call in flight.

Very long, low body, with egg-shaped head. Scarlet bill high at the base. Adult male white with smooth, green-glossed head.

Female bright silvery gray with rusty head and white chin; compact crest. In flight, both sexes show large square white wing patches.

Red-breasted Merganser

Mergus serrator

L 23″ | **WS** 30″ | **WT** 2.3 LB (1,060 G) | ♂ > ♀

The most marine of the mergansers, this slender, snake-necked, small-headed duck is a common migrant and winter resident on salt water; small numbers also pause in migration and may winter on the state's large lakes. This species is likely to be seen from November to March at any coastal site, including Sandy Hook, Shark River, Barnegat Light, Avalon, and Cape May.

Another very quiet species, displaying male Red-breasted Mergansers can occasionally be heard to give a soft whining whistle.

Long, slim body with slender neck and small head with wispy crest. Slender red-orange bill appears upturned. Adult male with dark breast, white collar, crested green head.

Female dingy gray-brown with reddish-brown, crested head and only slightly contrasting chin. In flight, white wing patches in both sexes.

Ruddy Duck

Oxyura jamaicensis

L 15″ | **WS** 18.5″ | **WT** 1.2 LB (560 G) | ♂ > ♀

This chunky, large-headed, long-tailed duck is locally common in winter on freshwater marshes and estuaries; a few breed in the northern part of the state. Ruddy Ducks can be found from November to March at the northern reservoirs, Liberty State Park, the North Shore ponds, Brigantine NWR, and Cape May; breeding birds are seen most easily in the Meadowlands.

Ruddy Ducks spend much of their time sleeping in phlegmatic clusters of up to several dozen. Courting males, in bright rusty summer plumage, utter a soft, hollow, bubbling burp.

Fat, oval body with long tail, large head, and large, scooped bill. Dark cap and white cheek. Unlike other ducks, male's bright plumage is worn in summer rather than in winter.

Female's pale cheek crossed by dark line. Both sexes show dark wings in fast, buzzing flight.

Brown Ducks

To identify female ducks, young ducks, and male ducks in
dull summertime dress, begin by narrowing the possibilities.
Obvious streaking and mottling in the plumage indicates
a "dabbling" duck (pages 10–27), while "diving" ducks
(pages 28–44) tend to be uniformly dark, often with white
patches. Dabblers feed with heads submerged and tails
held high; divers swim below the surface.

Useful features include wing pattern and head shape,
both generally resembling those of the adult male. The long
tail is a good clue for Wood Ducks, Hooded Mergansers,
and Ruddy Ducks. On flying birds, look at the belly color: pale,
for example, in Green-winged Teal, darker in Blue-winged.

Coarse body markings typical of
dabbling ducks. Round or oval head,
blotched orange bill, and white-
bordered blue patch on wing distinguish
this Mallard from similar species.

Solid dark browns and blacks
characteristic of most diving ducks.
Pointed head, white-banded bill,
and blackish back of this Ring-necked
Duck unlike scaup or Redhead.

Wild Turkey

Meleagris gallopavo

♂ **L** 46″ | **WS** 64″ | **WT** 16.2 LB (7,400 G)

Hunted out of New Jersey by the mid-nineteenth century, our heaviest land bird is once again a common inhabitant of open forests and woodland edges. These huge, richly colored, long-tailed and tiny-headed birds are most easily found in central and southern New Jersey or in the forests of the northwest, including High Point State Park, but turkeys show up anywhere in the state, even in urban parks.

The male's loud, liquid gobbling is identical to that of barnyard turkeys. Females have a rich repertoire of clucks and cackles.

Very large, oval body with long, broad tail and naked head and neck. Plumage glistening bronze and black, with barred wings and chestnut-tipped tail. Male droops wings and fans tail in display.

Female slightly smaller, with less colorful head and smaller "beard" on breast. Both sexes may roost high in trees; flight is startlingly loud.

Ring-necked Pheasant

Phasianus colchicus

L 21" (ADULT ♂ TO 35") | **WS** 31" | **WT** 2.5 LB (1,150 G) | ♂ > ♀

This large, colorful, very long-tailed chicken is a local and usually uncommon resident of agricultural land and overgrown fields anywhere in the state. All North American pheasants are introduced; New Jersey's are regularly replenished by the release of captive birds.

Pheasants eat everything from waste grain to eggs, and in some parts of their range, they have been implicated in the decline of ground-nesting native birds.

Males court with a loud, harsh *hronk-hronk*, followed by whirring wingbeats. Females utter various chicken-like clucks.

Stocky body with long tail and small head. Male with bronzy body, green head, and red wattles; often a broad white ring on neck.

Female heavily barred and mottled. Both sexes largely terrestrial, but fly short distances with strong, loud wingbeats.

Red-throated Loon

Gavia stellata

L 25″ | **WS** 36″ | **WT** 3.1 LB (1,400 G) | ♂ > ♀

Pale-faced and slender, the Red-throated Loon is an abundant fall migrant and common wintering bird all along the New Jersey coast. From November to March, a look offshore can find the ocean sprinkled with the silvery dots of roosting and feeding loons; close looks can often be had at Sandy Hook, Barnegat Light, or, especially, at Avalon in October, when thousands pass in migration. Small numbers are regularly seen inland in spring and fall on the northern reservoirs.

Red-throated Loons are usually silent in winter.

Large; long, low-slung gray body. Slender neck and smoothly rounded head ending in slender bill, often held above the horizontal.

Spring birds may show rusty foreneck of breeding plumage. In flight, short, pointed wings; hunched back and small feet.

Common Loon

Gavia immer

L 32″ | **WS** 46″ | **WT** 9 LB (4,100 G) | ♂ > ♀

Large, dark, and blocky-headed, Common Loons are fairly common migrants and uncommon winter birds on the coast and large bodies of water inland. Less social than Red-throated Loons, they can be found offshore anywhere on the coast and seen at close range at Barnegat Light, Sandy Hook, or Spruce Run. Large numbers pass Avalon each fall. A few non-breeding birds are scattered across the state in the summer.

The weird screams and whistles for which this species is famous are occasionally heard even in winter.

Very large and dark, with short, thick neck and angular head. Bill thick and dagger-like, usually held horizontal.

Dramatically spangled breeding plumage in late spring. In flight, short, pointed wings; hunched back and large feet.

Pied-billed Grebe

Podilymbus podiceps

L 13″ | **WS** 16″ | **WT** 1 LB (450 G) | ♂ > ♀

Chunky, big-headed, and nearly tailless, the Pied-billed Grebe is a common winter resident on brackish impoundments and freshwater ponds and lakes; a few pairs breed most years in freshwater marshes. Winter birds are easily found on the North Shore ponds and northern reservoirs or at Brigantine NWR. Look for scarce breeders at Great Swamp NWR, the Sussex County marshes, or along Delaware Bay.

The call, most commonly heard in spring and summer, is a loud, hollow, low-pitched *pkow-pkow-powpowpow*.

Rotund, with thick neck and egg-shaped head. Fluffy white rear covers inconspicuous tail. In winter, chin dull white and short, thick bill ivory.

Breeding birds have black throat, vertical black band across silvery bill.

Horned Grebe

Podiceps auritus

L 14″ | **WS** 18″ | **WT** 1 LB (450 G)

Lean and long-necked, the Horned Grebe is a common migrant and winter resident on the coast, with a few pausing on migration on large inland lakes. Unlike its freshwater cousin the Pied-billed Grebe, this species is often seen in flight, when its slender shape and white wing patches identify it. Horned Grebes are easily found from November to March from Sandy Hook to Cape May and well up into Delaware Bay. They are silent in winter.

Flat-backed and long-necked, with short dark bill. Winter birds elegantly black and white, with bright foreneck and face.

Breeding birds with rust-red neck and sides, golden tufts on side of crown. White wing patches and large feet in flight.

Northern Gannet

Morus bassanus

L 37″ | **WS** 72″ | **WT** 6.6 LB (3,000 G)

True birds of the sea, Northern Gannets are common and conspicuous migrants and winter residents on the coast and in Delaware Bay; a few, mostly immatures, spend the summer off the New Jersey shore. Peak migration is in November and April, when hundreds or thousands of these huge, long-winged, pointed-tailed aerialists stream past Sandy Hook, Avalon, Cape May, and other coastal points. At a distance, stiff, shallow wing beats and spectacular plunging dives distinguish them from gulls.

Very large, with long pointed wings, long pointed tail, and long head and bill. Full adults with white back, black wing tips, golden-tinged head.

Juveniles brown above, gradually whiter with age. Unlike gulls, stiff, mechanical wing beats.

Brown Pelican

Pelecanus occidentalis

L 51" | **WS** 79" | **WT** 8.2 LB (3,740 G) | ♂ > ♀

As more southerly populations recovered in the late 20th century, Brown Pelicans moved into New Jersey, where they are now fairly common summer visitors as far north as Island Beach State Park. Small groups can often be seen flying very slowly, single-file, low over the water off Cape May, Stone Harbor, and other coastal sites from May to September. Successful nesting seems inevitable, but no records as of 2013.

Very large, with heavy, bulbous body, long neck, small head, and very long bill. Juveniles dull brown-gray with paler underparts.

Adult plumage, acquired at 3–4 years, with rich brown neck, white crown and "racing stripe." Upper bill pale pink-tan.

Double-crested Cormorant

Phalacrocorax auritus

L 33″ | **WS** 52″ | **WT** 3.7 LB (1,700 G) | ♂ > ♀

Still uncommon in New Jersey just fifty years ago, the archaic-looking Double-crested Cormorant is now an abundant migrant and winterer across the entire state and a fairly common breeder on reservoirs, rivers, and bays. Fall migration sees up to a quarter million cormorants moving south in long, wavering lines past Avalon, and this species is hard to miss at any time of year on the northern reservoirs or at the Meadowlands, Sandy Hook, Brigantine NWR, or Cape May.

Cormorants give only the occasional soft grunt.

Heavy body with long tail, long neck, and long hooked bill. Adults glossy black with bare orange throat and face.

Long tail, stiff wing beats, and occasional gliding distinguish cormorants from geese in flight.

Great Cormorant

Phalacrocorax carbo

L 36″ | **WS** 63″ | **WT** 7.2 LB (3,300 G)

Another rapidly increasing seabird, the large, heavy-billed Great Cormorant is fairly common in winter on the coast. This lethargic species greatly prefers saltwater, but migrants are occasionally seen flying overland or pausing on large lakes and reservoirs; a few winter on the Delaware River south of Trenton. Reliable sites from November to March include Sandy Hook, Barnegat Light, Stone Harbor, and Sunset Beach in Cape May, where cormorants roost on the wreck of the concrete ship.

Very heavy body with medium-length tail; thick, "lumpy" neck; and thick hooked bill. Adults black with dull yellow throat bordered white. Thighs white in breeding plumage.

Very thick neck and heavy head distinguish from Double-crested in flight. In young birds, dark neck and breast contrast with paler, buffy-white belly; young Double-crested Cormorants generally show the opposite pattern, with a pale neck and breast and blackish belly.

American Bittern

Botaurus lentiginosus

L 28″ | **WS** 42″ | **WT** 1.5 LB (700 G)

This heavy, secretive heron is far less often seen than heard; the distinctive spring song is a low-pitched, hollow, gulping *BOK-ka-powp,* usually given at night from dense freshwater or brackish marshes. Discovered on the ground, bitterns often "freeze," bills skyward, in the attempt to blend in with the surrounding cattails or reeds. In flight, blackish wingtips contrast with brown body; green toes often dangle.

Now very scarce, American Bitterns can be found in the breeding season at Great Swamp NWR; migrants are most often seen at Brigantine NWR and Cape May.

Large, stocky, and short-legged, with bulky, tubular neck and small head. Cryptically patterned brown plumage with heavily streaked neck.

Least Bittern

Ixobrychus exilis

L 13″ | **WS** 17″ | **WT** 2.8 OZ (80 G)

Tiny, slender, and reclusive, Least Bitterns are uncommon breeding birds of extensive, heavily vegetated wetlands across the state. They are sometimes seen perched precariously on reed stems, but like the much larger and stockier American Bittern, they are usually detected by their weird song, a hooting chuckle *poo-poo-poo*. When feeding, Least Bitterns pace slowly along the ground or stand still with the slender neck fully extended. In flight, strikingly large buffy wing patches contrast with the black (male) or rich brown (female) back. This species is most often found in the Meadowlands and at Cape May.

Very small and fairly long-legged, with relatively slender, streaked neck and dark cap. Solid brown or black above with paler wings, especially obvious in flight.

Great Blue Heron
Ardea herodias

L 46″ | **WS** 72″ | **WT** 5.3 LB (2,400 G) | ♂ > ♀

Our most familiar heron, especially in freshwater habitats, the large and lanky Great Blue Heron is a common permanent resident across New Jersey; numbers are highest in late summer, when many birds move north after breeding and a dozen or more can be seen hunting large marshes and lakeshores. Like other herons, this species is active day and night, and individuals and small groups are often seen high overhead at dawn and dusk flying with distinctively slow, deep wingbeats to distant feeding areas. The Great Blue Heron's feeding style is sedate: birds stand patiently for long periods before striking into the water for a fish or frog. Especially in winter, they can also be seen hunting on land, where they take rodents and other prey on farm fields.

Often vocal in flight, Great Blue Herons croak out harsh, low-pitched belching calls.

Very large, long-necked and long-legged heron with oval head and thick, dagger-like bill. Adult with dull blue body and pale pink neck, striking black and white head.

Juvenile with dark crown, white throat, and streaked neck. Rusty thighs at all ages.

Head and neck drawn back in flight; long toes may dangle. Two-toned upper wing.

Great Egret

Ardea alba

L 39″ │ **WS** 51″ │ **WT** 1.9 LB (870 G) │ ♂ > ♀

The recovery of the Great Egret is one of America's conservation successes. Gone from much of its range by 1900, this largest of New Jersey's white herons is now a common breeder and visitant across the state; a few linger in the south in mild winters. Numbers are highest in late summer, when many can be seen at the Meadowlands, Brigantine NWR, Cape May, and inland wetlands.

Great Egrets are slow and patient hunters, standing for long periods in deep water. Calls are low croaks.

Long legs and broad wings. In flight, curled neck creates angular bulge below line of body. Slow, even wingbeats are easily counted. Bones of wing often visible as dark shadows on underwing.

Very large size, snaky neck, yellow bill, and long black legs and feet distinctive. Long, loose plumes on lower back in breeding plumage. Slow and methodical feeding behavior, standing perfectly still and waiting for prey.

Cattle Egret

Bubulcus ibis

L 20″ | **WS** 36″ | **WT** 12 OZ (340 G)

Short-legged and squat, the lawn-loving Cattle Egret arrived
in North America from Africa in the 1940s. By 1980 one of New
Jersey's most abundant herons, it has since become scarce and
probably no longer breeds in the state. Cattle Egrets spend
most of their time on dry land, hunting insects on pastures
and fields, but flock with other herons at roost and in nesting
colonies. They are most likely to be seen on agricultural land
near Delaware Bay.

Cattle Egrets are usually silent.

Small and chunky, with short neck,
jowly head, yellow bill, and
short, dull yellow to blackish legs.
Breeding adults with buffy-orange
on crown, breast, and back.

Short neck and short, dull-colored legs.
Wingbeats fast and decisive, unlike floppy
beats of other herons.

Snowy Egret
Egretta thula

L 24″ | **WS** 41″ | **WT** 13 OZ (360 G)

Compact and elegant, the medium-sized Snowy Egret, once hunted nearly to extinction for its delicate plumes, is once again a common summer visitor to New Jersey's coastal marshes, where some nest. Though occasionally seen inland, Snowy Egrets are most abundant in tidal wetlands; particularly large numbers can be seen in summer at the Meadowlands, Brigantine NWR, and Cape May. Snowy Egrets are often frenetic hunters, chasing their prey through shallow water. Calls are hoarse rasps.

Medium-sized, with relatively thick neck and round head. Bill black with yellow-orange at base, toes yellow. Airy plumes in breeding season.

Relatively short legs and wings. In flight, curled neck creates smooth bulge in line with rest of body. Yellow toes can be covered with mud.

Little Blue Heron

Egretta caerulea

L 24″ | **WS** 40″ | **WT** 12 OZ (340 G)

Fairly common but inconspicuous, the Little Blue Heron is a thick-set, saturnine bird of New Jersey's southern marshes. Late summer sees a few birds, mostly white juveniles, visiting inland lakes and ponds, but the best places to look for this species are coastal sites such as Brigantine NWR, Nummy Island, and Cape May. Little Blue Herons are very quiet when hunting, standing motionless with outstretched neck for long periods. The infrequently heard call is a low-pitched grunting croak.

Medium-sized, with thick neck and flat head. Thick bill gray with black tip, legs greenish gray. Adult slaty with dull purplish neck.

Juvenile white with small dark wing tips; older immatures patched slaty and white. Greenish legs, thick black-tipped yellowish or gray bill.

Green Heron

Butorides virescens

L 18″ | **WS** 26″ | **WT** 7 OZ (210 G)

The short-legged, thick-necked, richly colored Green Heron is the smallest and least social of our common herons. Though this species breeds in freshwater wetlands across the entire state, it is secretive and usually solitary, keeping to deep shade along ponds and riverbanks, where it hunts slowly and methodically, often with neck outstretched and tail twitching nervously. Occasional individuals roost in leafy suburbs far from water. Green Herons can be found from April to September at Kearny Marsh, the northern reservoirs, Brigantine NWR, and many other wetland sites. They are often first detected by their distinctive call, a very loud, explosive *kKow*.

Small and egg-shaped, with thick neck. White on throat and neck; colorful legs. Adult with blue-green wings and back, purplish neck and dark crown.

Crow-like at distance, but long bill and protruding yellow or orange toes.

Juvenile with spotted wings and white on throat and neck. Much smaller than night-herons.

Black-crowned Night-Heron
Nycticorax nycticorax

L 25″ | **WS** 44″ | **WT** 1.9 LB (870 G)

True to its name, the heavy-set, somber-looking Black-crowned Night-Heron is most active in the dark; glimpsed at dusk or dawn, the large head, round wings, and relatively swift wing beats can make this species look surprisingly owl-like in flight. During the day, night-herons are most often seen roosting sullenly in small groups in low trees over water. This species is a fairly common breeding bird and migrant in coastal marshes and on larger lakes inland. It is reliably seen at Brigantine NWR, Nummy Island, and Cape May; a few winter at scattered locations, where they often allow close approach.

The high-pitched, hollow, hoarse quacking call *quork* is infrequently heard during the day, but is a characteristic sound of nighttime marshes.

Fat, with short legs, thick neck, and long bill. Adult with black back and crown, dove-gray wings.

Juvenile with large white spots above, much greenish-yellow on bill and face.

Short legs barely visible beyond tail; rounded wings create owl-like appearance.

Yellow-crowned Night-Heron

Nyctanassa violacea

L 24″ | **WS** 42″ | **WT** 1.5 LB (690 G)

Largely nocturnal, the elegant, relatively slender Yellow-crowned Night-Heron is a scarce and inconspicuous breeder in southern coastal woodlands; post-breeding wanderers, most of them brown juveniles, can appear anywhere, but are most frequently observed in quiet salt marshes at dusk and dawn. Stone Harbor, Nummy Island, and Brigantine NWR are good places to look for this bird in summer, and late in the season, as many as twenty birds, including young juveniles from a nearby colony, can often be seen in the Meadowlands marshes of Carlstadt and Secaucus.

The infrequently heard call, *quenk,* is higher-pitched and less hollow than that of the more vocal Black-crowned Night-Heron.

Relatively slender, with longish legs, fairly thin neck, and short, stout bill. Adult with pale gray body and strikingly black and white head.

Young bird with small white spots on wings, plain face, and short, thick black bill.

Long legs extend noticeably beyond tail in flight.

Tricolored Heron

Egretta tricolor

L 26″ | **WS** 36″ | **WT** 13 OZ (380 G)

The slender-necked, fine-billed, and contrastingly marked
Tricolored Heron is a rare and declining breeder in southern
coastal New Jersey and a rare post-breeding visitor to marshes in
the north; it is by far the scarcest of the "expected" herons inland.
Often tame and conspicuous, this species is most readily found
at Brigantine NWR, Cape May, and, especially, Nummy Island.
Tricolored Herons are more active while hunting than Little
Blue Herons but more sedate than Snowy Egrets; they prefer the
edges of tidal channels and creeks. Calls are low and grating.

Medium-sized, with thin
neck and very long, thin bill.
White belly and underwing
distinctive. Adults pale
blue-gray; rusty plumes on
back in breeding season.

Long legs and slender
neck make this contrastingly
marked species the most
attenuated of all our herons.
Juvenile with rusty sides
of neck and wing edgings;
pattern of white and dark
otherwise like that of adult.

Glossy Ibis
Plegadis falcinellus

L 23" | **WS** 36" | **WT** 1.2 LB (550 G) | ♂ > ♀

The bizarrely beautiful Glossy Ibis, with its shimmering plumage and long, downcurved bill, is an uncommon but conspicuous summer resident of southern salt marshes, where loose flocks feed in the tidal mud with herons and waterfowl. From April to September, this species is easily observed at Brigantine NWR, Stone Harbor, Cape May, and other coastal wetland sites; a few may be seen in late summer inland. Usually silent, but may give a low, buzzing quack.

Long-bodied and thin-necked, with very long, downcurved bill. Breeding adult with white lines bordering gray face; juveniles browner, streaked white.

Skinny neck extended in flight, long legs trailing. Strong, decisive wingbeats alternate with gliding.

Black Vulture

Coragyps atratus

L 25" | **WS** 59" | **WT** 4.4 LB (2,000 G)

Almost unknown in New Jersey before the 1980s, the large, distinctively short-tailed and square-winged Black Vulture is now a common resident across the state, often seen soaring with Turkey Vultures. The two species often roost together in groups numbering in the hundreds. Most abundant along the Delaware River, this species can also be reliably found at Cape May and other hawk watch sites. Black Vultures may hiss, but are usually silent.

Large but compact, with very short tail, square head, and long, hooked bill. Bare head blackish, legs gray. Often tamer than Turkey Vultures, Black Vultures regularly perch on low posts or on the ground.

Short, square tail; square white patches in wings. Fast, shallow flapping makes wing beat seem to "twinkle." In mixed flocks, often fly higher than Turkey Vultures.

Turkey Vulture

Cathartes aura

L 26″ | **WS** 67″ | **WT** 4 LB (1,830 G)

Abundant and familiar throughout the state, huge, brown-black Turkey Vultures are most often seen soaring high in small groups. Their distinctive shape, with very long, pointed wings, ample and tapered tail, and tiny head, distinguish them immediately from other large birds. Nighttime roosts, which often include Black Vultures, can number in the hundreds of birds. Nesting birds may hiss, but this species is otherwise silent.

Very large and long-bodied, with long wings and tail. Feet pinkish; adult's tiny head red, juvenile's gray-black.

Long, two-toned wings held up in shallow V. Tips from side to side in flight; infrequent wing beats slow, very deep. In mixed flocks, often fly lower than Black Vultures.

Osprey
Pandion haliaetus

L 23″ | **WS** 63″ | **WT** 3.5 LB (1,600 G)

Very large and brightly marked, the Osprey was nearly exterminated from the eastern US in the mid-twentieth century; with a decrease in pesticide use, this species is once again a common breeder in New Jersey's coastal marshes and a common migrant throughout the state. Pairs nest in trees and on bridges, pilings, and nest platforms all along the state's Atlantic Coast and on the Delaware Bayshore north to Salem County, with smaller numbers on large reservoirs. Easily seen from March to October at Sandy Hook, Brigantine NWR, and Cape May. Calls are loud, clear whistles.

Very large; long-winged and small-headed. Rich brown above, bright white below, with dark stripe on white head. Juveniles spangled white above.

Long, bicolored wings; wingtip held down. Flies with loose, heron-like wingbeats; gathers twigs for messy, bulky nest.

Bald Eagle
Haliaeetus leucocephalus

L 31″ | **WS** 80″ | **WT** 9.5 LB (4,325 G) | ♀ > ♂

New Jersey now hosts more than 100 nesting pairs of this huge, stolid bird of prey, testimony to the species' recovery after it had been devastated by pesticides and shooting. Numbers of migrants and wintering birds have also increased, and Bald Eagles are an almost expected sight along the Delaware River and Bay, or at Brigantine NWR, Cape May and other hawk watches, and the northern reservoirs. They are often vocal in late winter, giving scratchy falsetto cackles from a perch or in flight.

Huge, with barrel-shaped body; medium tail; large, fluffy head; and long bill. Adult with white head and tail, yellow bill.

Immature's underwing blotched white; head and tail gradually whiten with maturity.

Very long, rectangular wings; long neck, large head and bill.

Northern Harrier

Circus cyaneus

L 18″ | **WS** 43″ | **WT** 15 OZ (420 G) | ♀ > ♂

Long-winged, long-tailed, and buoyant, the elegant Northern
Harrier hunts low over New Jersey's winter farm fields and
wetlands. Wintering birds often form communal roosts.
Migrants are common at all of the state's hawk watches; from
August to April, this species is usually easy to find at Alpha,
Brigantine NWR, Cape May, and along the Delaware Bayshore.
A few still linger to breed in the state's southern salt marshes,
especially in Atlantic and Cumberland Counties. Quiet in
winter, but nesting birds give a thin whistle and a high, light
chatter *klekleklek*.

Slender, with long legs, long
wings, and long, narrow tail.
Adult male usually silver
with dotted white underparts.

Most active at dawn and dusk; flattened, owl-like face directs sound to ears. Juvenile bright rusty below.

Long, narrow wings held in shallow V. From beneath, blackish inner wing contrasts with paler outer wing. Female streaked on white breast.

Sharp-shinned Hawk

Accipiter striatus

L 11″ | **WS** 23″ | **WT** 5 OZ (140 G) | ♀ > ♂

This short-winged, small to medium-sized hawk is a common migrant and winter resident across New Jersey and a rare breeding bird in deciduous forests, especially in the northwest. Sharp-shinned Hawks specialize in hunting birds up to the size of starlings and flickers, which they fearlessly chase down in flight. High Point and Stokes State Forest are the best sites in summer, while migrants can be seen, sometimes in very large numbers, at any of the hawk-watch sites in April and September. In winter, they hunt the edges of woodlands and suburban yards, often frequenting bird feeders. Migrants and winter birds are silent, but breeders in their display flight give a high-pitched, slightly nasal cackle.

Small (males) to medium-sized (females). Small, rounded head steep forehead, large eye, smal bill. Adults brownish to bluish above, underparts reddish.

Short, rounded wings held slightly forward. Moderately long tail, short neck and head.

Full chest, moderately long barred tail, slender legs. Juvenile with coarse brown or reddish streaking below.

Cooper's Hawk
Accipiter cooperii

L 16.5″ | **WS** 31″ | **WT** 1 LB (450 G) | ♀ > ♂

Rapidly increasing across its range, this short-winged, medium-sized hawk is now a common migrant and winter resident across New Jersey and an uncommon breeding bird in forests, agricultural landscapes, and wooded suburbs statewide. Cooper's Hawks take birds up to the size of pigeons, which they chase down in flight. Individuals of this very bold species are often seen in backyards, where they may splash in birdbaths and hunt prey at feeders; breeding birds can be aggressive, flying low and fast at intruders. This is a vocal raptor, especially in the breeding season, when adults produce a low-pitched, metallic chant *kek-kek-kek*.

Medium-sized. Angular head with steep nape, sloping forehead, and large bill. Long tail. Adults brownish to bluish above, underparts reddish; dark cap.

Fairly short, rounded wings held straight out from body. Long tail, long neck and head.

Lanky body, long barred tail, thick legs. Juvenile with fine brown streaking below.

Broad-winged Hawk

Buteo platypterus

L 15″ │ **WS** 34″ │ **WT** 14 OZ (390 G) │ ♀ > ♂

This rather small, tame, pointed-winged hawk is a very
common spring and fall migrant and a local and unobtrusive
breeder in woodlands statewide. Except when migrating,
Broad-winged Hawks tend to stay within their preferred
forests, where they hunt from low, inconspicuous perches.
Migrants, sometimes gathered into "kettles" of hundreds of
birds, are seen in April and in September and October; they
tend to be more abundant inland, and the hawk watches at
Chimney Rock, Montclair, and Merrill Creek can be especially
rewarding. Nesting birds are regularly found at High Point and
Worthington State Forest and in the Pine Barrens. The call is a
distinctively high-pitched, rather steady whistle *peEER*.

Juvenile streaked and
splotched brown below;
heavy face pattern.

Fairly small and stocky, with large head and often hunch-backed posture. Adult with reddish barring on underparts, heaviest on breast.

Fairly short, pointed wings held flat when soaring. Underwing pale; adult tail with broad black and white bands.

Red-shouldered Hawk

Buteo lineatus

L 17″ | **WS** 40″ | **WT** 1.4 LB (630 G) | ♀ > ♂

The neatly marked Red-shouldered Hawk, once one of the most common birds of prey in eastern North America, is now an uncommon migrant and wintering bird and an endangered nesting species in New Jersey. In the breeding season, this is a retiring bird of wooded wetlands, only infrequently seen soaring like the larger, much more abundant Red-tailed Hawk; Great Swamp NWR, High Point, and Stokes State Forest are good places to look. Migrants are more conspicuous, and can be seen reliably in October and November at most of the state's hawk watches. Summer Red-shouldered Hawks are most often detected by their loud vocalizations, a series of pure, keening, downslurred whistles.

Medium-length, rounded wings held slightly forward, wing tips often held down. All ages with pale bar across wing tip.

Medium-sized, with long neck, legs, and tail. Adult with black and white wings; densely barred reddish beneath. Black tail with thin white bands.

Red-tailed Hawk

Buteo jamaicensis

L 19″ | **WS** 49″ | **WT** 2.4 LB (1,080 G) | ♀ > ♂

Large, heavy, and powerful, the Red-tailed Hawk is one of the most common, and the most familiar, of New Jersey's raptors. Frequently seen perched on roadside trees and poles, Red-tailed Hawks are also master aerialists, pairs often soaring together high in the sky. They occur in all but the most densely wooded habitats, from open farm country and salt marshes to city parks and suburban back yards; nests are often conspicuous in tall trees. An abundant migrant at all of the state's hawk watches in October and November, this species is also common in all but the snowiest winters. The call is a distinctively harsh, descending screech *HYEEoww,* given at all seasons.

Large, with heavy, tubular body, long wings, and relatively short tail. Back bordered buff-white; underparts white with black streaking concentrated on lower breast. Adult with coppery tail.

uvenile tail brown
o dull red, with well-
paced black bars.

ong, somewhat pointed wings
eld out straight from body.
Underwing with narrow black
ar on leading edge; square
ale patches at wingtip.

Rough-legged Hawk

Buteo lagopus

L 21″ | **WS** 53″ | **WT** 2.2 LB (990 G) | ♀ > ♂

The Rough-legged Hawk, the largest of the long-winged soaring hawks, is a very uncommon migrant and winter resident especially in the northern half of New Jersey; a few pass Cape May and other hawk watches in November. Decidedly an open-country species, Rough-legged Hawks avoid forested habitats in favor of agricultural fields and marshes, where they are most active at dawn and dusk. Wallkill NWR, Manahawkin, and Jakes Landing can be good places to look for this species.

Large, with long wings and tail and small head and bill. Tail usually white at base, with one or more dark bands.

Most New Jersey winterers solid dark with paler wings; rarer light birds hav̶ solid black belly.

Raptor Identification

Hawks can be fast-moving and shy, and many have no striking plumage characteristics. The largest, eagles and ospreys, are often obviously large and long-winged. Smaller soaring hawks, or buteos, (pages 82–88) have broad, long wings and short, fan-shaped tails; the sprinting hawks, or accipiters, (pages 78–81) are short-winged and long-tailed.

Precise proportions and shapes of the wing and tail are often enough for identification: Sharp-shinned Hawks, for example, are shorter in all dimensions than the otherwise similar Cooper's Hawk. Some buteos have unique tail patterns, or distinctively shaped pale patches in the wing. Also note such flight habits as hovering or soaring with wings held above or below the horizontal.

Short, rounded wings and long, narrow tail typical of accipiters. Small head, squared tail tip, and slight "crook" in the wing rule out Cooper's in favor of Sharp-shinned Hawk.

Buteos have long wings and short, broad tails. Juvenile Red-tailed Hawks such as this have brown tails, but the stocky shape and square pale "windows" near the wing tip identify them.

Clapper Rail
Rallus longirostris

L 14.5″ | **WS** 19″ | **WT** 10 OZ (290 G) | ♂ > ♀ #

Abundant and noisy, the large, dull-colored Clapper Rail is a very secretive summer resident of coastal salt marshes, where it feeds on the ground in dense vegetation and is heard far more often than seen. Only at low tide do these long-billed rails emerge onto the mud of tidal creeks and flats; otherwise, listen for their decrescendo series of loud, hollow knocks and grunting squeals at Brigantine NWR, Jakes Landing, and Tuckerton.

Chicken-sized, with long, slightly downcurved bill. Dark above, dull gray and buff below with barred sides. Long legs dangle in infrequent flight.

Virginia Rail

Rallus limicola

L 9.5″ | **WS** 13″ | **WT** 3 OZ (85 G) | ♂ > ♀

Usually no more than a voice in the cattails, the Virginia Rail is a dapper, brightly colored summer resident of freshwater and brackish marshes. Half the size of the Clapper Rail, Virginia Rails are fairly common at Great Swamp NWR, Trenton Marsh, and Dividing Creek; a few may winter where there is unfrozen fresh water. Common calls, all higher and sharper than those of the Clapper, include a stuttering *k'dik k'dik,* a long descending series of nasal grunts, and well-spaced ticking notes.

Small and richly colored, with long, downcurved red bill. Orange breast contrasts with gray face and black and white flanks.

American Coot

Fulica americana

L 15.5″ | **WS** 24″ | **WT** 1.4 LB (650 G) | ♂ > ♀

Hundreds of these clunky gray rails gather each winter on ponds, lakes, and large rivers throughout New Jersey, lingering until the water freezes. Versatile foragers, they dive or skim vegetation from the surface, and often emerge to graze on lawns, displaying their greenish legs and grotesquely scalloped toes. A few pairs breed in northern marshes, but American Coots are most easily seen between October and April on the northern reservoirs and North Shore ponds and at Brigantine NWR and Cape May. Social but fractious, squabbling coots give a variety of weird, shrill clucks and chatters.

Heavy-bodied and thick-necked, with conical white bill. Slaty gray with white undertail.

Dull green legs. Toes with floppy lobes. Fine white trailing edge on wing visible in flight.

Common Gallinule
Gallinula galeata

L 13″ | **WS** 22″ | **WT** 8 OZ (235 G) | ♂ > ♀

Superficially similar to the larger, heavier American Coot, the elegant Common Gallinule is an uncommon and usually retiring summer resident of densely vegetated marshes; it is more common in the southern part of the state than in the north, and more frequently encountered in Delaware Bayshore wetlands than on the coast. Look and listen for this bird from May to early September in Sussex County marshes, in the Meadowlands, at Mannington Marsh, and at Pedricktown.

Most active at dawn and dusk, Common Gallinules give a wide variety of shrill, trumpet-like calls, heard even at night.

More slender and more secretive than coots, with smaller head and dark bill, horizontal white line on flank.

Adult with red bill, juvenile with dull dusky orange. Holds wingtips raised over back when swimming.

Black-bellied Plover

Pluvialis squatarola

L 11.5″ | **WS** 29″ | **WT** 8 OZ (240 G)

This large-headed and rotund shorebird is a common migrant
and winter visitor on New Jersey's beaches; a few immatures
can often be found in summer. Loners by shorebird standards,
Black-bellied Plovers associate loosely with Sanderlings,
turnstones, and Purple Sandpipers, but only rarely form large
flocks. Always alert and sometimes shy, this can be the first
species to fly when an intruder approaches. The frequently
heard call is a loud, mellow, slurred whistle *peeYURup*.

Fat-bodied, with square
head and large bill. In
flight, white tail and wing
stripe. Breeding adult
with silvery upperparts and
black breast.

Juvenile and non-breeding
adult speckled yellowish-
white above. Off-white
below with smudgy breast.

American Golden-Plover

Pluvialis dominica

L 10.5″ | **WS** 26″ | **WT** 5 OZ (145 G)

An uncommon migrant from August to November and rare in spring, the long-winged, dark-plumaged American Golden-Plover occurs on coastal mudflats and inland fields, often in association with Black-bellied Plovers, from which it is distinguished by its slightly smaller size, shorter bill, and muted wing and tail patterns. Sandy Hook and Brigantine NWR are good places to look, but the largest flocks typically occur on inland fields after storms; sod farms and ball fields are favored habitats. The flight call is a soft, slightly scratchy, ascending whistle *tchreeUP.*

Plump, with long wings and small head. Legs longer, bill shorter and finer than in Black-bellied. Dark cap sets off white eye stripe.

Breeding adult with dark spangled upperparts, black underparts and face. In flight, dark tail, dull gray-brown wings with poorly defined whitish stripe.

Semipalmated Plover

Charadrius semipalmatus

L 7.25″ | **WS** 19″ | **WT** 1.6 OZ (45 G)

Small and round, the strikingly patterned Semipalmated Plover is a common migrant on beaches and in salt and freshwater marshes. In April and May and from July into October, this species can be seen running along the sand and mud at Sandy Hook, Barnegat Light, Brigantine NWR, Stone Harbor, and Cape May; it is slightly less common but reliable, especially in fall, on inland lakeshores. The flight call is a loud, slightly screeching whistle *chREEp*.

Round-bodied and round-headed, with short, bicolored bill. Mud-brown above with black neck ring and face markings, paler in juvenile.

Short, broad wings and large head. Dark rump and upperparts with bold white wing stripe.

Piping Plover
Charadrius melodus

L 7.25″ | **WS** 19″ | **WT** 1.9 OZ (55 G)

The Piping Plover is a scarce migrant and declining breeder
on sandy beaches from Sandy Hook to Cape May, where
its eggs and young are threatened by careless vacationers. Even
adults are hard to detect against the pale backgrounds
they prefer, but from March to October they can be reliably
seen at Island Beach State Park, Stone Harbor, and Cape
May. The distinctive call, given in flight and from the ground,
is a soft, breathy, two-noted *PEE-po*.

Pudgy, with large head
and very thick bill.
Sand-brown above with
complete or broken
neck ring and pale face.

Pale above and below,
with whitish base of tail.

Killdeer

Charadrius vociferus

L 10.5″ | **WS** 24″ | **WT** 3.3 OZ (95 G) | ♀>♂

Large, long-tailed, and noisy, this abundant resident of open landscapes is New Jersey's most familiar shorebird. Killdeers breed on farm fields, parking lots, and even gravel roofs, where their bold patterns break up the bird's silhouette to let them go unnoticed by predators. If a nesting Killdeer is discovered, it often engages in a dramatic distraction display, drooping its wing, displaying its colorful tail, and crying piteously to draw the intruder away. Large flocks can be seen in July and August on fields and sod farms; a few winter on ponds and rivers as long as there is open water. Calls include rapid trills, stuttering screeches, and long, repeated whistles *deer deer deer*, all with a distinctive nails-on-the-blackboard quality.

Large, with very long tail and wings creating strongly horizontal impression. Two black breast and neck rings, strongly marked face, long, dark bill.

Often flies high overhead, calling. Bright white below, boldly patterned above with long wings and tail, broad white wing stripe.

Downy chick has only one breast band.

American Oystercatcher
Haematopus palliatus

L 17.5″ | **WS** 32″ | **WT** 1.4 LB (630 G) | ♀ > ♂

The large, stocky, comical American Oystercatcher is a common breeding bird in extensive salt marshes and on coastal beaches, where a few also winter. Cape May, Stone Harbor, Brigantine NWR, and Sandy Hook are reliable spring and summer sites, while wintering birds are frequent at Barnegat Light. Often quite tame, oystercatchers usually prefer to walk away from disturbance; when they do fly, it is with even, powerful wing beats and far-carrying piping calls like a referee's whistle.

Very large, with angular body, thick legs, staring eye, and long, red, chisel-shaped bill.

Black and white tail, broad white wing stripes. Often first detected by loud, penetrating calls.

American Avocet

Recurvirostra americana

L 18″ | **WS** 31″ | **WT** 11 OZ (315 G)

Pot-bellied, small-headed, and long-legged, the American Avocet is a scarce summer and fall visitor to southern New Jersey's coastal marshes. Usually encountered as single individuals or in very small groups, these conspicuous birds sometimes linger for days or weeks at the same site; look for them from July to November at Brigantine NWR or Cape May, where they can be seen standing quietly in the shallows or sweeping the water with their extremely fine, upturned bills. The ringing metallic *klee-klee-klee* calls are rarely heard from migrants and wanderers.

Tall but fat, with long neck and legs and small, round head; bill long, thin, and upcurved. Mostly white, with bold black and white upperparts; pink neck and breast in breeding adults.

Often loaf with head tucked for hours at a time, but very energetic when feeding, rushing ahead and waving bill back and forth through shallow water.

Spotted Sandpiper

Actitis macularia

L 7.5″ | **WS** 15″ | **WT** 1.4 OZ (40 G)

Long-tailed and small-headed, the Spotted Sandpiper is
a common breeder on freshwater ponds and riverbanks
throughout the state; migrants can be found in late spring
and late summer at any wetland edge, from tidal salt
marsh to parking lot puddles. Brigantine NWR, Great Swamp
NWR, and any small wetland with muddy edges are good
places to look. The constant teetering of feeding birds and
low, direct flight on stiffly vibrating wings are distinctive, as
is the slightly scratchy, upslurred call *pit-TWEET*.

Small, with long rear end,
oval body, and tiny head.
Breeding adults with yellow
legs and bill base, lavishly
spotted underparts.

Bright white belly of
juveniles and non-breeding
adults extends as "spur"
in front of wing. Long white
wing stripe in flight.

Solitary Sandpiper
Tringa solitaria

L 8.5″ | **WS** 22″ | **WT** 1.8 OZ (50 G)

The somberly colored, elegantly proportioned Solitary
Sandpiper is a fairly common migrant on wooded ponds and
inland mudflats, where it walks with high steps and delicately
bobbing head. Usually encountered in only small numbers,
birds can be found in May and August at Great Swamp NWR,
Trenton Marsh, and Walker Avenue Wetlands. Unlike most
freshwater shorebirds, this is a shy species, and it is often not
detected until it flushes with deep, swooping wingbeats and
clear, relatively even-pitched calls *pee-pseet*; the call is often
heard at night during migration. In flight, Solitary Sandpipers
are very dark, with distinctive blackish underwings and nearly
unmarked upperparts; the dark-centered tail is conspicuously
barred black and white on its outer edges.

Small, with dark, faintly
spotted upperparts
and white eye ring; barred
outer tail. Legs and
bill base dull gray-green.

Greater Yellowlegs
Tringa melanoleuca

L 14″ | **WS** 28″ | **WT** 6 OZ (160 G)

Relatively large, bulky, and heavy-billed, the Greater Yellowlegs is a common migrant and scarce winter visitor in coastal marshes; smaller numbers also pass inland. From March to May and from late July to October, this active and conspicuous species can be found readily at Sandy Hook, Brigantine NWR, and Cape May. Its distinctive call is a loud, metallic, heavily accented *woo-TOO-to*, given on flushing or in flight high overhead.

Sturdy, with full breast, muscular neck, and long, pale-based bill. Dark upperparts boldly spangled (adults) or speckled (juveniles) white; adult's white underparts coarsely and extensively marked black.

Thick neck and large bill obvious in flight. Finely barred white tail. Long, heavy yellow legs.

Lesser Yellowlegs

Tringa flavipes

L 10.5" | **WS** 24" | **WT** 2.8 OZ (80 G)

The Lesser Yellowlegs is a fairly common migrant coastally and inland in April and May and from late July to September. Smaller, slenderer, and darker- and shorter-billed than the Greater, it is also less frenetic when feeding, rarely swimming or splashing through the shallows. The thinner neck, smaller head, and shorter bill make it much less front-heavy in flight than Greater. The infrequently given call is a quiet, musical, flat *do-do* or *do-do-do,* given on flushing.

Slender, with thin, short neck and short, dark bill. Dark upperparts boldly spangled (adults) or speckled (juveniles) white; adult's white underparts with sparse black markings.

Short-billed and "neckless" in flight. Finely barred white tail. Long, thin yellow legs.

Stilt Sandpiper

Calidris himantopus

L 8.5″ | **WS** 18″ | **WT** 2 OZ (58 G) | ♀ > ♂

Tall, slender, and long-billed, the Stilt Sandpiper is a fairly common August to October migrant on coastal mudflats, often in association with yellowlegs and dowitchers, both of which it resembles. This species is told from yellowlegs by its duller legs; thicker, drooping bill; and pronounced eye stripe. It differs from dowitchers in its slim body, long wings, and shorter bill. Stilt Sandpipers feed with methodical vertical motions, tipping their tails high in the air.

Medium-small and elegant, with long wings, long greenish-yellow legs, and thick, slightly downturned bill. Adults with reddish cheek patch and barring below.

Juveniles neatly patterned black, white, and rust above. In flight, toes protrude beyond whitish tail.

Willet

Tringa semipalmata

L 15″ | **WS** 26″ | **WT** 8 OZ (215 G)

Relatively large and decidedly stocky, Willets are common in salt marshes on the Atlantic and lower Delaware Bay. They are easily observed at Brigantine NWR, Nummy Island, and Jakes Landing. Breeding birds arrive in April and stay until August, when their place is gradually taken by larger, less heavily marked migrants from western North America; a few may overwinter on southern beaches. Nesting Willets are very noisy; perched birds give a nervous, tern-like *klip*, while displaying birds sing a ringing, breathy *plill-will-willet* in flight.

Blocky shape, with thick body, thick bill, thick legs. Eastern breeders brownish, with heavily marked underparts in summer. Bill and legs dull gray or green.

Striking wing pattern above and below. Western migrants and winterers grayer and less distinctly marked, with longer bill.

Red Knot
Calidris canutus

L 10.5" | **WS** 23" | **WT** 4.7 OZ (135 G) | ♀ > ♂

Uncommon and rapidly declining, this plump, short-legged, and stout-billed sandpiper migrates in small numbers along New Jersey's coasts. The largest concentrations are in mid-May on lower Delaware Bay beaches, where knots join other shorebirds feasting on horseshoe crab eggs. A few may winter with Black-bellied Plovers on jetties and beaches at Barnegat Light, Brigantine Island, or Cape May. Knots are tame when feeding and roosting. The whitish rump and tail are obvious in flight.

Chunky, with short neck and round head. Short, dark bill and stout, olive-gray leg Breeding adults robin-red below and on face.

Winter adults undistinguished gray with white eye stripe; juveniles with lacy feather edgings above.

Ruddy Turnstone
Arenaria interpres

L 9.5″ | **WS** 21″ | **WT** 3.9 OZ (110 G) | ♀ > ♂

The rotund, bright-legged, and short-billed Ruddy Turnstone is a common winter denizen of rock jetties, which it shares with Sanderlings, Dunlins, and often Purple Sandpipers; large numbers can be seen in May feeding on horseshoe crab eggs along the lower Delaware Bay. Winter birds can reliably be seen at Manasquan, Barnegat Light, and Cape May. This is a lethargic and tame species, spending most of its time loafing or picking slowly through the seaweed, and only reluctantly flushing with a low, growling rattle *du-du-du-du*.

Stubby body with square head; short, orange legs and pointed bill. Dark bib sets off white breast patch and throat.

Complex black and white wing pattern, white tail with black band. Upperparts bright rust in breeding plumage.

Dunlin
Calidris alpina

L 8.5″ | **WS** 17″ | **WT** 2.1 OZ (60 G)

The dark and chunky Dunlin is one of the most common migrant and wintering sandpipers on New Jersey's coast, where dense flocks feed and roost in salt marshes and on mudflats, beaches, and rocky jetties. From late September to May, Dunlins are hard to miss at the Manasquan Inlet, Barnegat Light, Brigantine NWR, and Stone Harbor. Adults in full breeding plumage are seen in May; otherwise this is our most uniformly brown sandpiper above, the dark head and breast creating a hooded appearance. Loafing Dunlins seem neckless and short-legged; in flight, they are browner than Purple Sandpipers, and show white in the outer tail. Usually quiet on the ground, Dunlins give a variety of low, growling calls in flight.

Small, with short black legs and thick, obviously down-curved black bill. Full belly and breast, large head with short, thick neck.

Breeding adults with bright rust on back, black on belly, whitish face.

Often in dense, incredibly maneuverable flocks, shifting to alternate dark brown upperparts and flashing white underparts.

Sanderling

Calidris alba

L 8″ | **WS** 17″ | **WT** 2.1 OZ (60 G) | ♀ > ♂

Small, round, and perpetually in motion, Sanderlings are the most familiar of our coastal sandpipers. Sanderlings are easily seen on sandy beaches at Sandy Hook, Barnegat Light, and Cape May, where they may be present year-round; they are most abundant in winter, when flocks of these sturdy whitish birds run furiously along the surf edge. Pressed too close by humans or gulls, Sanderlings flush with musical chirping calls, showing bright, broad wing stripes before landing nearby.

Fat, with large round head and tubular black bill. Trips along wet sand on black, three-toed feet. Winter birds and young pale, with dark shoulder mark.

Breeding adults variably brown to reddish above and on breast and face. All birds show broad white wing stripe in flight.

Purple Sandpiper

Calidris maritima

L 9″ | **WS** 17″ | **WT** 2.5 OZ (70 G) | ♀ > ♂

A locally common winter resident of rocky, surf-washed jetties, the squat, dark Purple Sandpiper joins Dunlins and Ruddy Turnstones from October to early May at Manasquan Inlet, Barnegat Light, and Cape May. Lethargic and often very tame, Purples perch low in the rocks, hunched over their orange legs. If flushed, they fly in tight formation, settling nearby and huddling together in the dim nooks of the jetty.

Medium-sized and dumpy, with small head, short orange legs, and thick, orange-based bill. Blackish upperparts and dark gray breast create junco-like appearance. In flight, all dark above, including outer tail feathers.

Sorting Shorebirds

Shorebird flocks may contain more than one species. When such a flock appears, pay attention first to size and wing length; particularly small or particularly large birds, or especially stumpy or especially elegant individuals will stand out immediately. Pay close attention to the width and extent of wing stripes and to the patterns of rump and tail; no two shorebird species show exactly the same amount of white.

Semipalmated Sandpiper

Calidris pusilla

L 6.25″ | **WS** 14″ | **WT** 0.88 OZ (25 G) | ♀ > ♂

Our most common small migrant sandpiper, the Semipalmated Sandpiper is a tiny, gregarious bird of open mudflats; it is especially abundant at Brigantine NWR, Nummy Island, Heislerville, and Cape May, but can be found in often large numbers at any marsh or muddy pond, inland or coastal, in May and again from late July to October. Flocks are often noisy, giving a range of low-pitched chirping and grunting calls while perched and in flight.

Very small, with relatively short wings; short, blobby-tipped bill; and medium-length dark grayish legs. Breeding adults with black spangles above and contrasting dark cap.

Juveniles neatly scaled above, sometimes with bright reddish tones. Underparts sparsely marked. Tubular blunt-tipped bill.

Western Sandpiper

Calidris mauri

L 6.5" | **WS** 14" | **WT** 0.91 OZ (26 G) | ♀ > ♂

In spite of its name, this species is a common fall migrant on New Jersey's coast, with small numbers wintering most years from Brigantine NWR south to Cape May. Adults arrive in late July, followed three or four weeks later by juveniles; often flock with Semipalmated Sandpiper in migration. Breeding-plumage birds have extensive reddish edges on back and rusty cheek and crown. Juveniles show cold gray back and grayish wing panel separated by line of rusty scapular ("shoulder") feathers. Fuller, whiter breast than Semipalmated; slightly longer bill with pronounced droop at tip. Longer black legs are set back farther on the body, making Westerns appear less balanced and more front-heavy. Westerns often wade in deeper water than Semipalmateds, even submerging head. Infrequently given calls are high, thin, and scratchy.

Very small. Long, drooping bill and fairly long black legs. Breeding birds with rusty cap and spotted, streaky breast.

Juveniles with "zoned" pattern of gray back, rusty shoulder bar, grayer wing.

Least Sandpiper

Calidris minutilla

L 6″ | **WS** 13″ | **WT** 0.7 OZ (20 G)

The dark-plumaged, pale-legged Least Sandpiper is common and easily found in April and from late July to October at DeKorte Park, Brigantine NWR, Great Swamp NWR, and Walker Avenue. Their tameness, tiny size, and crouching posture make these birds inconspicuous on the drier, sparsely vegetated edges of mudflats and ponds they frequent. Extremely small and short-winged, Least Sandpipers give a repeated, rising *krrrreeep* in flight.

Tiny, with short wings, hunched posture, and fine-pointed, drooping bill. Adults very dark above, with coarsely streaked brownish breast.

Juveniles blackish above with reddish feather edges and thin white stripe on back. Legs dull yellowish (but often muddy).

White-rumped Sandpiper
Calidris fuscicollis

L 7.5″ | **WS** 17″ | **WT** 1.5 OZ (42 G) | ♀ > ♂

Often overlooked, the slender, neatly marked White-rumped Sandpiper is a fairly common fall and scarce spring migrant, especially coastally. Look for it August to October at Brigantine NWR, Stone Harbor, and Heislerville; fall storms often drive birds inland to Great Swamp NWR or sod farms. The long wingtip and relatively short, centrally-placed legs give this species a drawn-out, horizontal appearance unlike the smaller, stubbier Semipalmated Sandpiper.

nall, with wingtip extending beyond e tail. Black legs, slightly downturned lack bill with inconspicuous red ase. Adults finely streaked on breast nd flank. White rump in flight.

Pectoral Sandpiper
Calidris melanotos

L 8.75″ | **WS** 18″ | **WT** 2.6 OZ (73 G) | ♂ > ♀

The oddly shaped Pectoral Sandpiper is a common migrant on sparsely vegetated mudflats and sod farms, with particularly large numbers in April in the Pedricktown marshes; fall migrants are easily found August to October at Brigantine NWR, Cape May, and inland sites such as the Walker Avenue Wetlands. Noticeably larger than the small migrant sandpipers, Pectorals stand out with their long wings, deep bellies, and small heads. The flight call is a low-pitched, grumbling trill *brrrrp*.

Medium-sized and portly. Round back, deep belly, full breast, small round head with thick, slightly drooping bill; legs and bill base yellow. Streaked brown breast contrasts with white belly.

Long neck often stretched, making head look even smaller. Juveniles neatly scalloped black, white, and rust above.

Buff-breasted Sandpiper

Calidris subruficollis

L 8.25″ | **WS** 18″ | **WT** 2.2 OZ (63 G) | ♂ > ♀

This elegant, dove-like shorebird is a scarce August and September migrant on the coast and, especially, inland fields, often in the company of American Golden-Plovers and Black-bellied Plovers. Birds are seen each year at Sandy Hook, Brigantine NWR, and Cape May, but the largest numbers are usually found on sod farms in Salem County, where they feed with mincing steps and bobbing heads. In flight, the relatively broad wings flash white beneath.

Medium-sized. Long-winged and full-breasted, with long neck, often stretched, and small head. Bill thin and short; thin, relatively long yellowish legs.

Short-billed Dowitcher

Limnodromus griseus

L 11″ | **WS** 19″ | **WT** 3.9 OZ (110 G) | ♀>♂

Medium-sized and stocky, with a very long, slightly drooping bill, the Short-billed Dowitcher is a common and characteristic migrant shorebird of tidal marshes and mudflats. Large numbers can be found in April and May and again from July to September at Brigantine NWR, Nummy Island, and DeKorte Park; this species is rare in winter at those same sites, and scarce inland at any season. Dowitchers feed and roost in flocks of up to a few thousand individuals, often mixing with yellowlegs and other mid-sized shorebirds. They feed by walking slowly and methodically through shallow muddy water, dipping and raising their long bills vertically in a distinctive "sewing machine" motion. Quiet on the ground, Short-billed Dowitchers give a toneless, low-pitched, muffled *duh-duh-duh* in flight.

Medium-sized, with rather short yellowish legs and long, pale-based, slightly drooping bill. Breeding adults with dark cap, broad eye stripe, and usually white belly. Tail with broad white bars.

Juveniles with complex "tiger-striped" pattern above.

Broad, diffuse white trailing edge to wing and white "cigar" on lower back in flight.

Long-billed Dowitcher
Limnodromus scolopaceus

L 11.5″ | **WS** 19″ | **WT** 4 OZ (115 G) ♀ > ♂

Slightly larger and longer-billed than the Short-billed, the
Long-billed Dowitcher is an uncommon migrant and a rare
winterer on coastal mudflats and marshes, typically arriving
later and staying longer in the fall than its very similar relative.
The bulbous, hunch-backed shape and frequent high-pitched,
peeping calls are further distinctions. Long-billed Dowitchers
can be found starting in September at Brigantine NWR, Stone
Harbor, and Cape May.

Breeding adults extensively
reddish beneath, including
belly. Tail with narrow
whitish or reddish bars.

Juveniles with relatively
plain, rusty-fringed
upperparts.

Wilson's Snipe

Gallinago delicata

L 10.5″ | **WS** 18″ | **WT** 3.7 OZ (105 G) | ♀ > ♂

An inconspicuous, well-camouflaged migrant and winter visitor to heavily vegetated ponds, the Wilson's Snipe is seldom seen until flushed from almost underfoot, when it flies off in an erratic zigzag, calling a harsh, buzzing *skaip* and showing its long, pointed wings and rusty-orange tail. Snipe are most easily found in October and November at Great Swamp NWR, Trenton Marsh, and other grassy wetlands; large numbers are sometimes found in April at Pedricktown and other Delaware Bayshore sites. Wintering birds can occur wherever there is unfrozen water.

Medium-sized, with very long, straight bill. Cryptic brown and yellow pattern of back resembles dried vegetation.

Very long bill usually held pointed down. Bold stripes on back, white underparts.

American Woodcock

Scolopax minor

L 11″ | **WS** 18″ | **WT** 7 OZ (200 G) | ♀ > ♂

North America's most abundant shorebird, the tubby, long-billed American Woodcock is one of the most rarely observed, keeping to dark woodlands except when displaying or when driven to roadsides by snow. Displaying birds are easily seen at forest edges anywhere in the state on February and March evenings, first calling *brrzzpt* from the ground, then rising high in the sky to fall with a twittering, chipping song. Winterers are common in Cape May, where many are hit by cars in bad weather.

Large and fat, with big eyes and very long, straight bill. Cryptic brown and gray pattern of back resembles dried leaves.

Large and apparently tailless. Wings very short and, in flight, obviously rounded.

Shorebird Identification

New Jersey's three dozen regularly occurring shorebird species offer some of the state's most enjoyable birding challenges. Habitat often provides a first clue to identification. Solitary Sandpipers, for example, are typically found on small, wooded ponds; Lesser Yellowlegs are most common in salt marshes and on open flats. Semipalmated Sandpipers wade in shallow water, while Least Sandpipers prefer drier mud. Dowitchers feed methodically in the open, but the similar Wilson's Snipe lurks in the deep vegetation of marshes and roadside ditches.

Subtle but real differences in shape are also helpful: compare the slender, dove-headed American Golden-Plover with the blocky, huge-billed Black-bellied Plover, or the brutish necklessness of the Dunlin with the Western Sandpiper's more attenuated, more "normal" proportions.

The deep belly, small head, and long wing tips of this Pectoral Sandpiper distinguish it from other, superficially similar shorebirds.

This Least Sandpiper's plumage is very like that of a Pectoral Sandpiper, but note the stumpy wing and tail, thinner bill, and more evenly tapered body.

Bonaparte's Gull

Chroicocephalus philadelphia

L 13.5″ | **WS** 33″ | **WT** 7 OZ (190 G)

The tiny, gentle-faced Bonaparte's Gull is by far the smallest of our common gulls. This pale, long-winged, fine-billed gull occurs in sometimes very large flocks between November and April at coastal sites such as Sandy Hook, Barnegat Light, and Cape May; small numbers occur on large inland lakes. Very light and buoyant in flight, they can look like terns, but are distinguished by their squared-off tails and short, blunt bills. Hopeful observers always check winter flocks for rarer gulls.

Small but full-breasted. Breeding adult with neat slaty-black hood, reduced to small ear spot in winter. Orange feet, black bill.

Small and delicate, with narrow wings and short, black bill. Wing tip with long white wedge; immatures with brown M across wings and black tail band.

Laughing Gull

Leucophaeus atricilla

L 16.5″ | **WS** 40″ | **WT** 11 OZ (320 G) | ♂ > ♀

The noisiest summer bird of New Jersey's shore, the rakish Laughing Gull is familiar to all beachgoers. This dark, scimitar-winged species is abundant from late March to October from Sandy Hook to Cape May and well up Delaware Bay; hard to miss anywhere on the coast, it breeds in large numbers on Nummy Island, and wanderers are common on inland ponds and rivers everywhere but the forested Northwest. The familiar call is a very loud, nasal *weeaack-wuck-wuck-wuck*.

Dark and long-winged, with long, dark bill and snouty aspect. Wing tip above and below black, fading into dark gray. Young and non-breeding birds with dark shawl across neck.

Medium-sized and slender, with long wings extending well beyond tail. Long neck; dark, drooping bill. Breeding adult with black hood.

Lesser Black-backed Gull

Larus fuscus

L 21″ | **WS** 54″ | **WT** 1.8 LB (800 G) | ♂ > ♀

Very rare in the state before the 1980s, this dark, long-winged gull is now a regular cold-season visitor to ocean and bayside beaches and, especially, large rivers and reservoirs, where dozens may spend the winter. Cape May, Sandy Hook, Spruce Run, and Round Valley are good places to look, as are active landfills. Larger than Ring-billed Gulls, Lesser Black-backed Gulls are smaller and more slender than most Herring Gulls; perched, the wingtips extend far beyond the tail.

Slender, with long, narrow wings, small bill and head. White head contrasts with dark back and relatively uniform wings at all ages.

Adult dark slate above, with small white spots in wing tip. Yellow legs and bill with conspicuous red spot; winter adult with noticeable head streaking.

Great Black-backed Gull

Larus marinus

L 30″ | **WS** 65″ | **WT** 3.6 LB (1,650 G) | ♂ > ♀

The huge, broad-winged, and portly Great Black-backed Gull
is common year-round on sandy beaches and rock jetties; this
species is also easily found in winter on inland lakes and rivers
and at landfills. Look for these powerful gulls at DeKorte Park,
Sandy Hook, and Cape May, and on the large northern reservoirs.
Aggressive and voracious, they often capture and consume
live prey, including birds and mammals. The frequently heard
call is a very low-pitched, hollow, human-sounding *vrow-vrow*.

Barrel-chested and
stumpy-winged, with large
head and massive bill. White
head and breast contrast
with dark back at all ages.

Adult nearly black above,
with large white spots in
wing tip. Pink legs and huge
yellow bill; winter adult
with very little head streaking.

Herring Gull

Larus argentatus

L 25″ | **WS** 58″ | **WT** 2.5 LB (1,150 G) | ♂ > ♀

Large, bulky, and big-billed, the Herring Gull is the ubiquitous gull of the coast, abundant and gregarious at all seasons; Herring Gulls are also very common inland, especially in winter, often seen soaring high overhead on their relatively broad, pointed wings. Like all gulls, birds of this species go through a series of distinct plumages before reaching adulthood. They fledge into a rich, usually neatly speckled chocolate brown juvenile plumage; the silvery adult plumage is attained when the bird is three years old. All ages share a full breast, large, flat-crowned head, and long, thick, heavily angled bill. Bold around humans, Herring Gulls are aggressive among themselves; agitated birds give a wide variety of metallic or squeaking calls, including a low-pitched, resonant grunting *row-wow-wow-wow*.

Large and heavy, with broad wings, large head, and powerful bill. Neat juvenile plumage followed by messy brown and gray immature plumages, with broad dark tail band.

Stout, relatively short-winged. Juveniles handsome chocolate with neatly checkered upperparts; bill all dark at first, later with pink base.

Breeding adult silvery above with white head and breast, yellow bill with red spot. Winter birds heavily streaked and marbled brown on head and neck.

Ring-billed Gull

Larus delawarensis

L 17.5″ | **WS** 48″ | **WT** 1.1 LB (520 G) | ♂ > ♀

Medium-sized and elegant, the pale Ring-billed Gull is the common wintertime "seagull" of ponds, rivers, and fast food restaurant parking lots. Large numbers also winter on beaches with other gulls; a few, mostly immatures, linger over the summer, but this species is most abundant from September to April, when it is easily seen anywhere in the state, its squeaky, high-pitched *wa-wa* calls emanating from outside convenience stores in even the largest cities.

Pale and dainty, with rather narrow wings, small head, and relatively short, slender bill. Neat, thin tail band and extensive black in wing tip of immatures unlike Herring Gull at similar ages.

Long wings with considerable black; upperparts pale silvery gray. Breeding adult with white head, yellow legs, well-defined black band on yellow bill.

Black Skimmer

Rynchops niger

L 18″ | **WS** 44″ | **WT** 11 OZ (300 G) | ♂ > ♀

This extraordinary black and white seabird is the only North American species with the lower bill longer than the upper; skimmers use this feature to feed, snapping up fish as they fly low over the water with the lower bill parting the surface. An endangered species in New Jersey, skimmers breed colonially at Sandy Hook, Stone Harbor, and Brigantine Island, while hunting birds can be seen anywhere along the coast between April and November, including DeKorte Park. The call is a low-pitched, nasal quack.

ery long, pointed wings lack above, white below; lack neck and crown ith white forehead. Long, ompressed orange bill ith black tip.

Short legs, absurd bill. Juvenile speckled brown above; bill mostly dark and shorter than adult's.

Least Tern

Sternula antillarum

L 9″ | **WS** 20″ | **WT** 1.5 OZ (42 G)

Frenetic and noisy, tiny Least Terns are a familiar sight April to August on New Jersey's coasts, breeding in loose colonies on pale sandy beaches, where development and recreation threaten their survival. Their size and fast wingbeats can make them resemble small shorebirds in distant flight, but the pointed wings, forked tail, and habit of hovering and suddenly diving readily identify them. The distinctive and incessant call is a loud, squeaky, stuttering *p-tit*.

Very small, with forked tail, short pointed wings, and small sharp bill, yellow in summer.

Adult with inky cap and long white forehead. Outer wing with neat black wedge above.

Black Tern

Chlidonias niger

L 9.75″ | **WS** 24″ | **WT** 2.2 OZ (62 G)

The small, broad-winged, short-tailed Black Tern is an uncommon late summer and autumn migrant along the coast; adults arrive as early as July, while young birds appear from August to late September. This darkly exotic species, with its easy, fluttering and skimming flight style, should be looked for at Sandy Hook, Brigantine NWR, and Cape May; it typically feeds not by diving, like other terns, but by swooping low over shallow water to take prey from the surface.

Wings uniformly slaty above and below; short notched tail slightly paler, undertail white. Summer and fall adult patchy black and gray on head and breast.

Juveniles and winter adults dull whitish below, with dark "helmet" and "earmuffs," smudgy dark shoulder bar. Flight slow, easy, elegant; often very close to surface of water. Spreads tail and swoops down when prey is sighted.

Caspian Tern

Hydroprogne caspia

L 21" | **WS** 50" | **WT** 1.4 LB (660 G) | ♂ > ♀

The pterodactyl-like Caspian Tern is a common migrant and scarce breeder on New Jersey's coast, most often seen at Brigantine NWR; also look for it at DeKorte Park, Sandy Hook, Island Beach, Stone Harbor, and Cape May. Rare but regular inland, this species can also be seen at Mannington Marsh and the northern reservoirs, especially in late summer. Broad-winged, short-tailed, and heavy-billed, Caspian Terns may recall gulls, but the dark forehead at all seasons, very pale upperparts, and deep, rasping call *chrrrr* are distinctive.

Nearly as large as Herring Gull, with broad, pointed wings and shallowly forked tail. Solid dark or streaked black forehead, blackish wingtip from below.

Large and stocky, with carrot-shaped, black-tipped reddish bill. Wingtip gray above, blackish below.

Royal Tern
Thalasseus maximus

L 20″ | **WS** 41″ | **WT** 1 LB (470 G) | ♂ > ♀

The elegantly streamlined Royal Tern is a common seashore visitor July to October, when adults can be seen followed by squealing, begging young just off the beach at Sandy Hook, Barnegat Light, Stone Harbor, and Cape May. Almost as long as Caspians, Royal Terns are much slenderer, with narrower wings and longer, more deeply forked tails; the forehead is white except in spring and early summer. Adults give a musical bleating call, hungry juveniles a high, thin trill.

Long-winged and long-tailed, with relatively thin, pale-tipped orange-red bill. Forehead dark only in spring; wingtip blackish above, gray below.

Large and attenuated, with slightly curved bill. Unkempt crest at back of crown.

Common Tern

Sterna hirundo

L 12″ | **WS** 30″ | **WT** 4.2 OZ (120 G)

Nesting in colonies on sandy barrier beaches, the noisy, flamboyant Common Tern is present from late April to late September along the coast from Sandy Hook to Cape May. August sees an influx of migrants, a few of which also visit the large northern reservoirs and Delaware River. These long-winged, long-tailed birds dive for saltwater prey, often far off shore, where their pale plumage sparkles in the sea glare. Calls include an insistent, metallic *kip-kip-kip* and a grating, descending scream *KHyeeer.*

Narrow, sharply pointed wings with diffuse black wedge near wingtip; long, forked tail with narrow black outer edge. Breeding adult with pale gray underparts and red, black-tipped bill.

Juvenile and winter adult with dark bill, blackish half-hood, gray bar at "shoulder" of folded wing.

Forster's Tern

Sterna forsteri

L 13″ | **WS** 31″ | **WT** 6 OZ (160 G)

Less bound to sand and saltwater than the very similar
Common Tern, the long-legged, thick-billed Forster's Tern is
a common breeder in southern marshes and a very common
visitor April to October anywhere along the coast, especially
abundant at Brigantine NWR. This is the only tern likely to be
seen in winter, when small numbers often linger from Barnegat
Light to Cape May. Among this species' variety of calls is a very
low-pitched, growling *khaarr*.

Narrow, sharply pointed wings
with unmarked silvery wingtip;
long, forked tail with narrow
white outer edge. Breeding
adult with orange, black-tipped
bill, white underparts.

Longer legs, thicker
bill than Common Tern.
Juvenile and winter
adult with dark bill,
black mask through eye.

Rock Pigeon
Columba livia

L 12.5″ | **WS** 28″ | **WT** 9 OZ (270 G)

The familiar "city pigeon" is found in a feral state throughout New Jersey, most abundantly in urban settings, on farmland, and on beaches. Extremely variable in color, ranging from dull black to all white, Rock Pigeons are identifiable by their portly, small-headed shape; short, broad tail; and bright white underwing, conspicuous in flight. They walk with short, mincing steps and bobbing head. The song is a bubbling *hoohoohrooo*; courting birds also clap their wings noisily over their backs.

Fat, with short pink legs, thick neck, and small head and bill. Plumage variable, most commonly blue-gray with black bars across wing.

Broad, pointed wings; broad tail and small head. Underwing and usually rump white. Distant flocks identified by stiff wingbeat and variation in individual color.

Eurasian Collared-Dove

Streptopelia decaocto

L 13″ | **WS** 22″ | **WT** 7 OZ (200 G)

A recent addition to New Jersey's birds, the stocky, rather long-tailed Eurasian Collared-Dove has been seen along the coast north to Sandy Hook; the first breeding pairs were in Cape May, and the species can be expected to spread north into towns and agricultural areas. Often seen perched on wires or feeding quietly in small flocks beneath bird feeders and around livestock, this species is larger, paler, and shorter-tailed than the Mourning Dove. The song is a harsh, heavily accented *hoo-HOO-ha*; flying birds call *hurrRAAAY* on landing.

Medium-sized, with moderately long, square tail. Sandy overall, with unspotted wing, contrastingly dark wingtip, and neat black collar on nape.

Short, rather rounded wings with contrasting dark tip; square tail with white corners.

Mourning Dove
Zenaida macroura

L 12″ | **WS** 18″ | **WT** 4.2 OZ (120 G) | ♂ > ♀

Our only common native pigeon, the slender, long-tailed Mourning Dove is abundant over most of the state, breeding in habitats from forest edge and agricultural fields to suburbs and city parks; the nesting season extends over most of the year, with pairs regularly producing two or three broods each year. Smaller and slimmer than the Eurasian Collared-Dove, Mourning Doves are gray-brown, with conspicuously spotted wings. The wings produce a loud, musical, twittering whistle on takeoff. Mourning Doves are very fast in the air, sometimes twisting erratically as they fly on short, pointed wings; in sustained flight, each wing beat ends with a distinctive downward flick. The familiar song is a slow, measured, hooting whistle *oo-WAH-oo-ah-ah*.

Adult with powder blue eye ring. Pale pink and bronze iridescence on side of male's neck.

Medium-sized, with long,
pointed tail. Gray-brown, with
large black spots on wing;
pink legs and dark bill. Juvenile
with fine pale feather edges
creating scalloped appearance.

Very long tail held
closed to a point
in sustained flight; white
edges and corners
show when tail spread.

Yellow-billed Cuckoo

Coccyzus americanus

L 12″ | **WS** 18″ | **WT** 2.3 OZ (65 G)

The lanky and reptilian Yellow-billed Cuckoo is an uncommon breeder and common fall migrant in woodland edge and thickets, where it often sits silent and motionless. Stokes State Forest, Garret Mountain, Great Swamp NWR, Sandy Hook, and Cape May are reliable sites to find this species, which arrives in mid-May; fall migration begins in August and continues into early November. Vocalizations include a low, hoarse single hoot and a maniacal, decelerating chuckle *cow-cow-cow cow cow cow*.

Long-tailed and slender, with heavy, curved bill; lower bill and inconspicuous eye ring yellow. Large oval white spots on blackish undertail.

Black-billed Cuckoo

Coccyzus erythropthalmus

L 12″ | **WS** 17.5″ | **WT** 1.8 OZ (52 G)

Slightly smaller and usually less common than the Yellow-billed, the Black-billed Cuckoo is a quiet and secretive inhabitant of dark thickets and woods. Look for it at the same time and in the same places as the Yellow-billed. This species' vocalizations are softer, higher-pitched, and less startling; they include a gentle clucking *klow-klow-klow* and a soft, musical series of dove-like hollow whistles *coo-coo-coo*.

Long-tailed and slender, with short, slight bill. Eye ring red in adult, dull yellowish in young. Underparts off-white, tail spots small and gray.

Barn Owl

Tyto alba

L 16″ | **WS** 42″ | **WT** 1 LB (460 G) | ♀ > ♂

The ghostly pale, heart-faced Barn Owl, a victim of the suburbanization of New Jersey's agricultural landscape, is now a rare and infrequently seen resident of abandoned silos and industrial buildings. Migrants are occasionally detected in dense woodlands, especially conifers. Breeding birds are most readily found at Liberty State Park or the Meadowlands; migrants are often reported passing through the beam of the Cape May lighthouse, or detected by their weird rasping, hissing *shrkkk* overhead.

Very white in flight, with long, round-tipped wings. Flight erratic and bounding.

White, heart-shaped face with small oil-black eyes. Long legs and spotted underparts white to tawny buff.

Barred Owl

Strix varia

L 21″ | **WS** 42″ | **WT** 1.6 LB (720 G) | ♀>♂

Dark-eyed, puffy-headed, and somnolent, Barred Owls are very local residents of extensive dark forests. They are most readily seen—and far more often heard—at Great Swamp NWR, Stokes State Forest, and Belleplain State Forest. Barred Owls can be shy, but they are erratically active even in daylight, whooping their very loud, echoing barks *hoo-hoo hoo-HOOO* through tangled woodlands and swamps; other vocalizations include choking screams and siren-like whistles.

Fast, silent flight with stiff, decisive wingbeats. Wings and back with white spotting, short tail with narrow white bands.

Fluffy plumage, with rounded body and head. Dark eyes, yellow bill. Throat barred brown and white, belly streaked brown.

Eastern Screech-Owl

Megascops asio

L 8.5" | **WS** 20" | **WT** 6 OZ (180 G) | ♀ > ♂

New Jersey's most common owl, the compact, well-camouflaged, and deceptively cute Eastern Screech-Owl occurs wherever large trees provide suitable nesting cavities; this fierce predator also commonly inhabits nest boxes intended for Wood Ducks and other birds. The "ears"—tufts of feathers at the side of the crown—are often held down, giving the head a square appearance. The commonly heard call is a long insect-like trill; the "screeching" song is a stuttering, descending whistle *HEEEeeeee.*

Plumage varies from gray to brown to rusty red, independent of sex and age.

Very small and bark-patterned, with fierce pale eyes and large, feathered feet. Usually found sunning at entrance to tree cavity or nest box.

Great Horned Owl

Bubo virginianus

L 22″ | **WS** 44″ | **WT** 3.1 LB (1,400 G) | ♀ > ♂

New Jersey's largest, the massive Great Horned Owl is a common resident of dark woodlands with large trees, including city parks and suburban backyards, where it often goes undetected unless heard singing its mellow, syncopated song *hoo-hoo-hoo HOO hoo hoo*. A very early nester, adults are often on eggs in February, and young remain dependent on their parents for several months after leaving the nest, begging incessantly with a loud, grating *hweeep*.

Fast, silent flight with stiff, decisive wingbeats. Low-contrast mottled upperparts, inconspicuous tail barring.

Very large, with fireplug-shaped body and long feather "ears" at sides of crown. Eyes bright yellow, underparts finely barred, throat white.

Short-eared Owl

Asio flammeus

L 15″ | **WS** 38″ | **WT** 12 OZ (350 G) | ♀ > ♂

Perhaps the easiest owl to see in New Jersey, wintering Short-eared Owls, often in small groups, float moth-like over saltmarshes and farm fields from November to March; unlike other owls, this medium-sized, long-winged species is often active well before dark on overcast afternoons at such sites as Brigantine NWR, Jakes Landing, and Walkill NWR. The infrequently heard flight call is a coughing bark.

Medium-sized, with long wings and flat face. Rich buffy patch in outer wing; streaked breast contrasts with paler, unmarked belly.

Northern Saw-whet Owl

Aegolius acadicus

L 8″ | **WS** 17″ | **WT** 2.8 OZ (80 G) | ♀>♂

This common but rarely seen softball-sized owl winters in dense thickets throughout New Jersey; small numbers also breed in the Pine Barrens and forests in the Northwest. Strictly nocturnal, winter Saw-whets are usually detected only if discovered at roost deep in a low cedar or greenbrier tangle, but many are recorded in October and November passing south through Cape May and other coastal migration hotspots. Territorial birds in spring sing a slow, penetrating *toot toot toot* like the warning beeps of a backing truck.

Very small. Chocolate above with neat white spots, white below with broad buffy streaks. Glaring yellow eyes.

Chuck-will's-widow

Caprimulgus carolinensis

L 12″ | **WS** 26″ | **WT** 4.2 OZ (120 G)

Large, long-tailed, and expertly camouflaged, Chuck-will's-widows are fairly common breeding birds in coastal and southern pine forests. Strictly nocturnal, this species is usually seen only if accidentally flushed from the forest floor or glimpsed in the headlights along a Pine Barrens road. Look for Chuck-will's-widows and listen for their relaxed, whistled song *chuck prill PRIDDa* in May and June at Brigantine NWR, Belleplain State Forest, and Cape May.

Nearly pigeon-sized, with tail extending beyond folded wing. Usually reddish, brightest on tail and rump. Male with white edges to tail in flight.

Eastern Whip-poor-will

Caprimulgus vociferus

L 9.75″ | **WS** 19″ | **WT** 1.9 OZ (54 G)

Small, long-tailed, and expertly camouflaged, Whip-poor-wills are widespread but local and declining breeders in coniferous and deciduous woodlands in the southern half of the state. Strictly nocturnal, they are rarely seen unless stumbled across at a nest or roost. The song, an incessant, loud, hurried *hrip paWHILL,* can be heard from May to July at Brigantine NWR, Belleplain State Forest, and Cape May; a few are found farther north, at Stokes State Forest or High Point.

Roughly robin-sized, with tail extending beyond folded wing. Brown-gray overall, including rump and tail. Male with bold white corners to tail.

Common Nighthawk

Chordeiles minor

L 9.5″ | **WS** 24″ | **WT** 2.2 OZ (62 G)

Long, sharp-pointed wings with a white bar at the tip make
this insect-eater unmistakable as it darts with uneven
wingbeats above open fields, marshes, and city rooftops. Now
a rare breeder in the state, this species is still a fairly common
fall migrant, flocks of up to a few dozen moving south at dusk,
sometimes low, sometimes high overhead. Migrants are silent,
but summering birds give a loud, nasal, woodcock-like buzz;
their diving flight display ends with a startling whir produced
by the wings.

Long, narrow, pointed wings
crossed by white band; notched,
medium-length tail. Flight
uneven, deep wingbeats followed
by a flurry of shallow strokes.

Roosts on stump, post, horizontal
branch, or wire, often perched
crosswise. Upperparts gray,
underparts barred whitish. Folded
wing and tail of even length.

Chimney Swift

Chaetura pelagica

L 5.25″ | **WS** 14″ | **WT** 0.81 OZ (23 G)

Chittering flocks of these small, soot-colored, crescent-winged birds are a familiar sight over ponds and towns from April to October. Seriously declining as a breeder with the loss of nest sites in hollow trees and chimneys, swifts still gather in impressive autumn roosts in August and September; thousands swirl in to disused chimneys at schools and industrial sites in Ridgewood and the Meadowlands each year. The familiar call is a staccato *ptick*; courting birds soar on uplifted wings while giving a long, fast series of sharp notes.

Small and dark, with body tapered at both ends. Long, curved wings appear to beat alternately in flight. Very short, square tail ends in tiny spine-like protrusions, which help roosting birds cling to vertical surfaces.

Ruby-throated Hummingbird

Archilochus colubris

L 3.75″ | **WS** 4.5″ | **WT** 0.11 OZ (3.2 G) | ♀ > ♂

New Jersey's only common hummingbird is green-backed, with a fondness for bright flowers and sugar water. Arriving as early as March in the south, it is common throughout the state from April to October; fall migration begins in late July, when this species is especially easy to see hovering at feeders and wildflowers such as jewelweed and trumpet vine. The call is a metallic *tick*, often repeated. Hummingbirds seen after late October are likely to be one of the half dozen other, western or tropical species recorded in the state in winter.

Extremely small, with fairly long, forked tail and ridiculously small wings, blurred in flight. Adult male with dark throat, red in good light.

Young birds and female white-throated, often with hint of buff on flan

Belted Kingfisher
Megaceryle alcyon

L 13″ | **WS** 20″ | **WT** 5 OZ (150 G)

Noisy and flamboyant, the Belted Kingfisher is a common resident statewide; especially conspicuous in September migration, individuals winter as far north and inland as open water allows. Breeding birds are found wherever quarries, riverbanks, or road cuts expose steep slopes for excavation of nest cavities. The machine-gun-like rattle, shifting abruptly in tempo and pitch, can be heard at almost any pond, lake, or river, where kingfishers hunt from an exposed perch or by hovering, head and tail drooping, over their prey.

Fast but jerky flight, slow, deep wingbeats interrupted by faster bursts. Large head and bill often pointed downward.

Bulky and angular, with huge, crested head and long, dagger-like bill. Adult male lacks orange breast band of juveniles and adult female.

Red-headed Woodpecker

Melanerpes erythrocephalus

L 9.25″ | **WS** 17″ | **WT** 2.5 OZ (72 G)

The spectacularly tricolored Red-headed Woodpecker is a very scarce and local breeder in open forests in southern and northwestern New Jersey; look for it in Stokes State Forest, Great Swamp NWR, and Cape May NWR from May to September. A few migrants are seen in May and September along mountain ridges or at Cape May; in years with good acorn crops, a few winter in wet forests. This species' screams and rattles are harsher than those of the Red-bellied Woodpecker, recalling the hoarse calls of a gray squirrel.

Immatures blackish-brown, with white belly and large white wing patch crossed by brown bar.

Medium-sized, with round, bright scarlet head and chisel-like bill.

Rounded wings with flashing white patch on trailing edge.

Red-bellied Woodpecker

Melanerpes carolinus

L 9.25″ | **WS** 16″ | **WT** 2.2 OZ (63 G) | ♂ > ♀

Common and confiding, the red-capped, bluish-backed Red-bellied Woodpecker is a common resident of forests and wooded parks and suburbs throughout the state. Quiet in the breeding season, it is noisy and conspicuous the rest of the year, visiting feeders to gorge itself on sunflower seeds and suet. The loud calls include a wide variety of rattles and screeches, all with a cheerful, liquid quality unlike the hoarse rasps of the much rarer Red-headed Woodpecker.

Finely barred back bluish-gray, underparts tan with hint of orange on belly. Adult male with red cap and nape; females and immatures with less red.

Juvenile with gray head often slightly tinged red at nape; dull gray neck and underparts.

Hairy Woodpecker

Picoides villosus

L 9.25″ | **WS** 15″ | **WT** 2.3 OZ (66 G) | ♂ > ♀

A neat black and white resident of tall trees, the medium-sized Hairy Woodpecker is a fairly common but shy resident throughout the state, most often detected by its loud, sharp *peek* note and long, even-pitched rattle. Larger than the Downy and slightly smaller than the Red-bellied Woodpecker, the Hairy is often strikingly whiter on the underparts. In flight at close range, the stiffly beating wings make a distinctive popping noise.

Medium-sized, with stout bill. Back with central white stripe, head with two parallel straight white lines. Outer tail feathers white.

Downy Woodpecker
Picoides pubescens

L 6.75″ | **WS** 12″ | **WT** 0.95 OZ (27 G) | ♂ > ♀

Our smallest and, with the Red-bellied, our most common woodpecker, the familiar Downy occurs statewide in forests, parks, and backyards, where it often feeds close to the ground, even descending into pond-side reeds. It is a frequent and confiding visitor to feeders for seed and suet. The calls include a squishy, muffled *ptip* and a high, light, descending rattle. Downies often glide short distances between trees; in active flight, the wings are quiet.

Very small, with short bill. Back and underparts often dingy, outer tail feathers spotted black. Lower white stripe on head broadens markedly towards nape.

Northern Flicker

Colaptes auratus

L 12.5" | **WS** 20" | **WT** 4.6 OZ (130 G)

The large and strikingly colorful Northern Flicker is a common resident in open woodlands and suburbs throughout the state; impressive gatherings occur at Cape May and other coastal migration hotspots in early autumn. The most terrestrial of our woodpeckers, flickers are often seen feeding quietly on lawns and farm fields. The loud, slightly metallic spring song is an even-pitched *flick-ick-ick-ick-ick-ick*; other vocalizations include a startling downslurred *cleee-ear* and slow *wicka-wicka-wicka*.

Long wings and tail with bright golden undersurfaces. Flight steadier, less swooping or bounding than other woodpeckers.

Large, long-tailed, with evenly rounded breast and head. Barred above, spotted below, with red nape. Adult male with black moustache.

Yellow-bellied Sapsucker

Sphyrapicus varius

L 8.5″ | **WS** 16″ | **WT** 1.8 OZ (50 G)

Quiet and shy, the slender, long-winged Yellow-bellied
Sapsucker is a common April and October migrant throughout
the state and an uncommon winterer in mixed woodlands and
parks. It is a scarce but rapidly increasing breeder in High
Point State Park and Stokes State Forest. Tree bark in favored
locations is marked by regular matrices of shallow holes drilled
in search of sap. The rarely heard calls include weak, shrill
squeals and tinny rattles. Breeders hammer a loud, staccato
series of syncopated taps on dead wood.

Tube-shaped, with
small head and long
tail. Long vertical
white bar on black
wing, back mottled
white. Adult male
with red throat,
female with white.

White wing
patch at all ages.
Brown juvenile
plumage held
through winter.

Pileated Woodpecker

Dryocopus pileatus

L 16.5″ | **WS** 29″ | **WT** 10 OZ (290 G) | ♂ > ♀

Nearly crow-sized, the prehistoric-looking Pileated
Woodpecker is a fairly common resident of forests and well-
wooded suburbs; it is most easily found at High Point State
Park, in Stokes State Forest, and other extensive woodlands in
northwestern New Jersey, south to Mercer County. This species
feeds low in the trees, sometimes even on fallen logs. The calls
are flicker-like, but higher, less metallic, and more musical,
with exaggerated variations in pitch and tempo.

Very large, with striking
black and white pattern on
underwing, white flash
in upperwing. Deep, slightly
swooping wingbeats.

Very large, with long
tail and neck and
small, crested head.
Black back and
underparts. Adult male
with red moustache
and forehead; black
in female.

Monk Parakeet

Myiopsitta monachus

L 11.5″ | **WS** 19″ | **WT** 3.5 OZ (100 G)

Many parrot species have been reported "in the wild" in New Jersey, but only the green and gray Monk Parakeet has created permanent colonies. Bright, noisy, long-tailed exotics, escaped birds of this species have established small populations in several northern New Jersey cities; they are most easily found in Edgewater, where they build their bulky stick nests on roadside telephone poles and terrorize sidewalks and parking lots with their hoarse, raspy *kreeff.*

Medium-sized, with long tail and large head. Gray breast contrasts with green back and yellowish underparts.

Long, pointed or wedge-shaped green tail and blue-black outer wings. Zigzag flight, loud screeches from flocks of up to several dozen birds.

American Kestrel

Falco sparverius

L 9″ | **WS** 22″ | **WT** 4.1 OZ (117 G) | ♀ > ♂

A fairly common migrant and winterer in open habitats
from farm fields to industrial parks, the delicate, long-tailed
American Kestrel is now a very rare breeder in New Jersey.
Large numbers are seen in September at Cape May; winter
birds can be found at Sandy Hook, DeKorte Park, and Walkill
NWR. Kestrels hunt from short trees, poles, and wires, bobbing
their tails as they wait; they also hover skillfully. Breeding
birds are noisy, giving a clanging chant *klee-klee-klee*.

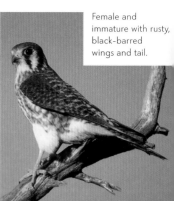

Female and
immature with rusty,
black-barred
wings and tail.

Small, with long tail and
pointed wings. Rusty
back, white face with two
vertical black streaks.
Adult male with blue
wings and black band
across rusty tail.

Impression in flight is of pale,
colorful, gracefully floating
bird with long wings and tail.

Merlin

Falco columbarius

L 10″ | **WS** 24″ | **WT** 6.5 OZ (190 G) | ♀ > ♂

Small, stout, and powerful, the Merlin is a common migrant and uncommon winter resident throughout New Jersey. Shorter-tailed and shorter-winged than kestrels, Merlins are fast and purposeful fliers, often little more than a dark streak as they dash past low over fields and marshes in search of small birds. Numbers pass Cape May and other coastal migrant hotspots in August and September; wintering birds are most easily found at Sandy Hook, Brigantine NWR, Stone Harbor, and other sites with shorebird concentrations.

Small, with relatively stocky wings and tail. Chocolate or dark gray back, pale gray face with single poorly defined moustache.

Fairly short tail, short but pointed wings. Overall dark, with narrow white bars across blackish tail.

Peregrine Falcon
Falco peregrinus

L 16″ | **WS** 40″ | **WT** 1.6 LB (720 G) | ♀ > ♂

Medium to large, the Peregrine Falcon is one of New Jersey's fastest birds, moving at great speed with a deceptively slow, shallow wingbeat as it hunts ducks and shorebirds on coastal mudflats and marshes; it is regularly seen inland as well. This species nests on cliffs, bridges, and specially installed platforms, and is easily seen at Palmyra, Brigantine NWR, and Fort Lee. Breeding birds give a low-pitched, quacking chant *kaa-kaa-kaa-kaa*. Migrants are common at Cape May in August and September.

Fairly large, with broad tail, full chest, and bulky shoulders. Barred or streaked beneath, with heavy black helmet and white cheek patch. Re-introduced coastal breeders may be very dark.

Broad, tapered tail and wide-based pointed wings. Uniformly colored below, with obscurely barred tail.

Great Crested Flycatcher

Myiarchus crinitus

L 8.75″ | **WS** 13″ | **WT** 1.2 OZ (34 G)

Boisterous and loud, but sometimes surprisingly difficult to see in the leafy trees it prefers, this large, puffy-headed, yellow-bellied flycatcher is a common forest bird throughout the state, arriving in May and lingering into September. Great Crested Flycatchers require large dead trees for breeding; they nest in old woodpecker holes and large birdhouses. The wide range of calls includes an upslurred whistle *wheep* and a croaking *raack-raack*.

Extensive rust on wing and tail conspicuous in flight. Innermost wing feathers with white edges.

Large and large-billed. Bright belly, smooth gray breast. Usually stays within woodland edge, hunting from large branches.

Eastern Wood-Pewee

Contopus virens

L 6.25″ | **WS** 10″ | **WT** 0.49 OZ (14 G)

The medium-small, long-winged, dingy-plumaged Eastern
Wood-Pewee is our most common woodland flycatcher,
inhabiting open forests with tall trees throughout the state
from May to September. Pewees perch conspicuously,
often at the tip of a dead branch, flying, often straight up, to
take prey from the air, then usually returning to the same
perch. Unlike the smaller flycatchers, this species does not flick
its shallowly notched tail, but vibrates it briefly on landing.
The distinctive vocalizations, heard on even the hottest summer
days, include a bright chip and a slow, heavily slurred series
of whistles *pee-a-WEE, PEE-urr.*

Sparrow-sized, with
slightly crested head,
long wingtip. Face plai
underparts dull gray,
low-contrast wingbars.

Willow Flycatcher

Empidonax traillii

L 5.75″ | **WS** 8.5″ | **WT** 0.47 OZ (13.5 G)

A small, gray-brown flycatcher of low, damp thickets and marsh edges, the Willow Flycatcher has a short, broad-based bill and fairly short wingtip. This species is fairly common but local over most of the state from May to August; its loud, sneezing, falling song *FITZbew* can be heard in the Meadowlands and at Great Swamp and Cape May NWRs. The lookalike Alder Flycatcher sings a rising *rrBEERa*; look for that species in shrubby marshes in northwestern New Jersey. The call of the Willow Flycatcher is a low, liquid *chlup,* while Alders give a sharp, high-pitched *peek*. Both flick the tail up.

Small, with large head, short wingtip; bill seen from beneath wide-based. Face plain, underparts off-white, wingbars neat whitish or brownish.

Acadian Flycatcher

Empidonax virescens

L 5.75″ | **WS** 9″ | **WT** 0.46 OZ (13 G)

The small, green-gray Acadian Flycatcher haunts dark mature forests from May to August; uncommon in the northwest at High Point and Stokes State Forest, it is most easily found at Belleplain State Forest, Glassboro, and other wet woodlands in the southern half of New Jersey. The startling song is an abruptly rising *pt-TSEET*; the call is loud and penetrating, resembling the distant *peek* of a Hairy Woodpecker. Flicks tail up.

Small, with large head, rather long wingtip; bill seen from beneath wide-based. Thin, well-defined whitish eye ring; pale underparts, bright wingbars.

Least Flycatcher

Empidonax minimus

L 5.25″ | **WS** 7.75″ | **WT** 0.36 OZ (10.3 G)

Small and neat, the big-headed, short-billed, chunky Least Flycatcher is the most familiar of New Jersey's small tail-flicking flycatchers. A common migrant in most wooded habitats statewide in late April and August and September, this species is fairly scarce as a breeder in the northwest; look for it at High Point, Stokes State Forest, and Walkill NWR. The call is a short, liquid *whit,* briefer and more decisive than that of the Willow; the song, commonly given in migration, is an irregularly spaced series of hurried two-noted phrases *ch'BEK.* Like other small flycatchers, this species flicks its tail nervously up.

Small, with long tail, small head, short wingtip. Bill seen from beneath short, narrow, and dark. Thin, well-defined whitish eye ring and bright white wingbars.

Eastern Phoebe

Sayornis phoebe

L 7″ | **WS** 10.5″ | **WT** 0.7 OZ (20 G)

Sluggish by flycatcher standards, the sparrow-sized Eastern Phoebe is a common migrant and breeder in open woods and parks across the state, arriving in March and departing in October; a few winter over in warm years. Nesting under bridges and eaves, phoebes are easily identified by their drab plumage and persistent slow tail dipping, unlike the trembling of pewees or the flicking of smaller flycatchers. The call is a sweet, loud chip. The familiar song is a lazy, buzzy, repetitive *fBEE, fbrreer*.

Sturdy and drab, with large head, medium tail, and short wings. Plain, dark face and dingy yellowish white underparts. In flight, dark, rounded wings and medium tail. Flight slow and fluttering.

Eastern Kingbird

Tyrannus tyrannus

L 8.5″ | **WS** 15″ | **WT** 1.4 OZ (40 G)

The noisy, charismatic Eastern Kingbird is a fairly common breeder on farmlands and woodland edges throughout New Jersey; look for it May to August perched on wires and low trees at Great Swamp and Brigantine NWR and in Salem County. August and September see a massive southward migration down the coast, especially impressive at Cape May, where flocks of hundreds can be seen. The distinctive call is a scratchy, thin *tzeer tzeer*, often accelerating into a frantic series.

Large and assertive, with broad, white-tipped tail and dark head setting off white chin and belly.

Dark, pointed wings and white-tipped tail; underparts bright white. Wingbeats often strikingly stiff and shallow, especially when calling.

White-eyed Vireo
Vireo griseus

L 5″ | **WS** 7.5″ | **WT** 0.4 OZ (11.5 G)

The chubby, brightly colored White-eyed Vireo is a common resident of southern New Jersey thickets from April to September; it is uncommon in the Northwest. The species is easily found at Cape May, Belleplain, and Brigantine NWR. White-eyed Vireos usually feed at the lower levels, but their fondness for dense vegetation makes them most readily detectable by their vocalizations, which include harsh wheezes and chatters and a lively, popping song *chip-cheWEERee-chip*; many individuals also mimic other songbirds.

Small, short-tailed, full-bellied, and round-headed. Greenish above, bright white and yellow below; neat, clear wingbars and bright yellow line connecting eye to bill.

Adult eye white (with black pupil); immature eye dark. Thick, gray feet typical of vireos.

Blue-headed Vireo

Vireo solitarius

L 5.5" | **WS** 9.5" | **WT** 0.56 OZ (16 G)

The handsome and hardy Blue-headed Vireo is a common spring and fall migrant throughout the state, passing through in April and again from September to November; a few breed in the cool, dark conifers of High Point State Park and other northwestern forests. Fearless and slow-moving, this species is usually easy to observe as it feeds methodically at low levels in trees and bushes. Blue-headed Vireos are readily located during migration at Garret Mountain, Palmyra, and Cape May and in city parks and suburban backyards. The frequent call is a harsh snickering *heghegheg*; the sweet, conversational song *vree vireo vereea* is heard on the breeding grounds.

Sparrow-sized, with short tail, thick body, and large head. Greenish above, blue-gray head. Broad wingbars, white spectacles on face.

Snowy throat; yellow flanks outlining white central underparts. Tail square-tipped.

Yellow-throated Vireo
Vireo flavifrons

L 5.5″ | **WS** 9.5″ | **WT** 0.63 OZ (18 G)

A colorful but retiring bird of the high treetops, the slow-moving Yellow-throated Vireo breeds locally in wet forests in the northern half of the state, with outliers in Cape May. This species arrives in early May and departs by September; look for it at forested sites such as High Point, Stokes State Forest, and Princeton. It is most easily detected by its song, a slow, lazy, buzzing *eeYAY, EEyeer*.

Sparrow-sized, with short tail, thick body, and large head Bicolored from beneath: white in rear, yellow in front. Broad white wingbars, wide yellow spectacles on face.

Red-eyed Vireo

Vireo olivaceus

L 6″ | **WS** 10″ | **WT** 0.6 OZ (17 G)

Our most abundant vireo, the subtly handsome, treetop-dwelling Red-eyed Vireo is often said to be the most common breeding songbird of the eastern US. Its muted green and gray plumage and deliberate habits make it difficult to see, but the song, a slow and insistent whistled chant *veero-veery*, is hard to miss from May to July in any mature woodland. This species is also a very common migrant throughout the state in August and September, when it can more often be found feeding lower in trees and bushes.

Sparrow-sized; tail fairly short. Upperparts soft green; flat head with gray cap outlined black. Whitish underparts often with yellow at side of breast.

Thick, hooked bill and stout gray feet distinguish vireos from warblers, kinglets, and other small greenish birds.

Warbling Vireo

Vireo gilvus

L 5.5" | **WS** 8.5" | **WT** 0.42 OZ (12 G)

A fairly common migrant and a local summer resident around forested lakes and river banks in the northern half of the state, the unassuming Warbling Vireo is more often heard than seen. Fond of the densely leaved tops of cottonwoods and willows, Warbling Vireos arrive in May and depart by September. In the breeding season, they can be found at High Point State Park, Great Swamp NWR, and Sandy Hook; fall migration, which begins in late July, brings them to any wooded area. In addition to typically whiny vireo calls, male Warbling Vireos sing a rising, raspy *zheery-eery-eery-eery-UP.*

Small, with medium-length tail and short, rather thick bill. Dull gray-tan above, paler below, with plain wings and broad, bland eye stripe.

Wide, arching eye stripe gives face a "startled" impression. May show faintly yellowish sides or breast, especially in fall.

Philadelphia Vireo

Vireo philadelphicus

L 5.25" | **WS** 8" | **WT** 0.4 OZ (12 G)

The colorful but retiring Philadelphia Vireo is a scarce fall migrant throughout New Jersey. In late August and September, single birds can occasionally be found at Sandy Hook, Palmyra, or Cape May, where they feed slowly and silently in dense tangles and trees, often in loose association with other vireos and warblers. Migrants seem to be attracted to fruiting shrubs such as dogwoods or honeysuckles, where they methodically pick insects from the leaves and fruits. This species is very infrequently heard in migration, but may give a soft, buzzy whine similar to the notes of other vireo species.

Small, with slightly longer tail and shorter bill than Warbling Vireo. Variably yellow on throat and breast, with duller belly and flank.

Wide, straight eye stripe gives face an "elegant" or "formal" appearance. Fine black line connects eye to base of bill. Gray cap contrasts subtly with greenish back.

Blue Jay
Cyanocitta cristata

L 11″ | **WS** 16″ | **WT** 3 OZ (85 G)

A bright, brash Mr. Hyde at wintertime bird feeders, the spectacular Blue Jay becomes a quiet and retiring Dr. Jekyll in the breeding season, when this common species withdraws inconspicuously into forests and wooded parks. Present year-round throughout New Jersey, southbound Blue Jays from farther north pass through the state in September and October, often streaming over in flocks of several dozen birds. The familiar calls include nasal screams, musical whistles, and quiet grunts.

Large white spots in rounded wing and tail. Flight slow and heavy, wings brought forward on each stroke.

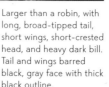

Larger than a robin, with long, broad-tipped tail, short wings, short-crested head, and heavy dark bill. Tail and wings barred black, gray face with thick black outline.

Common Raven

Corvus corax

L 24″ | **WS** 53″ | **WT** 2.6 LB (1,200 G) | ♂ > ♀

Very rare over much of the twentieth century, the huge, angular Common Raven is now a fairly common resident in northern New Jersey, and increasingly frequent as a visitor anywhere in the state. High Point, Stokes State Forest, and the northern hawk watches are dependable sites. On the ground, ravens move with a bouncing waddle, rolling the body to the side as they hop from foot to foot; in flight, they are masters of acrobatic grace, soaring effortlessly one moment and tumbling playfully the next. The varied calls include a deep, croaking *hrrukk*, wooden rattles, and gulping clucks.

Neck and head large, bill very heavy.

Very long, pointed wings and long, wedge-shaped tail.

American Crow
Corvus brachyrhynchos

L 17.5″ | **WS** 39″ | **WT** 1 LB (450 G)

American Crows are large, noisy, and gregarious residents throughout New Jersey, nesting in tall trees in parks and suburbs and on forest edges; they form roosts of up to several thousand birds in winter. Consummate omnivores, crows feed on everything from fruits and seeds to small birds and mammals, and loose flocks can be seen patrolling both farm fields and parking lots. Along with the familiar high-pitched *caw*, this species gives a wide range of croaking, rattling, and musical calls.

Much larger than a pigeon, with broad, square tail, long wings and heavy dark bill. Plumage glossy black.

Long, rounded wings moderately long, squared or rounded tail. Wingbeats powerful and fluid.

Fish Crow

Corvus ossifragus

L 15″ | **WS** 36″ | **WT** 10 OZ (280 G)

Slightly smaller than the American Crow, the nasal-voiced
Fish Crow is a common resident over all but extreme northwest
New Jersey; many leave inland sites to gather at the coast in
winter. Often found with American Crows, Fish Crows are best
distinguished by their thin, high-pitched calls *keh* or *kuh-uh*.
The two species have different molt schedules: a crow with
symmetrical gaps in the wing feathers in September or October
is likely a Fish Crow, while one showing such gaps in June is
an American Crow.

Slightly shorter wings,
slightly longer tail,
slightly faster wingbeat
than American Crow.
Gap in wing shows that
this bird is molting.

Horned Lark

Eremophila alpestris

L 7.25″ | **WS** 12″ | **WT** 1.1 OZ (32 G)

Rarely noticed in the open, windswept habitats it prefers, the sturdy, gregarious Horned Lark is a local and uncommon breeding bird and a common wintering species on farm fields and beaches. Nesting birds should be looked for on sod farms in central and southwestern New Jersey; wintering flocks are found feeding on the ground at Liberty State Park, Sandy Hook, and Barnegat Light. Flight calls are high-pitched and lisping, the song a thin, rising twitter *tink-tlinka-tloo*.

Sparrow-sized, with long black legs and moderately thick bill. Dull brown above, creamy below with black-patterned yellowish face.

Farm Country Birds

As forests have regrown and subdivisions have sprawled across New Jersey's landscape, the unkempt fields and pastures in which many of our most sensitive bird species nest have become ever scarcer. Today, such once-common open-country breeders as the Northern Harrier, the Bobolink, and the Vesper and Savannah Sparrows are officially listed as threatened or endangered in the state, making programs for the preservation of grasslands and farmlands more important than ever.

A rare fall migrant on fields and sod farms, the grass-loving Upland Sandpiper still breeds in tiny numbers— but only at sites closed to the public.

Big-billed and greenish-headed, an occasional Henslow's Sparrow attempts to breed in central New Jersey's farm fields, but the male's *ts'lick* song too often goes unanswered.

Purple Martin

Progne subis

L 8″ | **WS** 18″ | **WT** 2 OZ (56 G)

The dark, heavy-bodied, and broad-winged Purple Martin is our largest swallow, breeding in nest boxes and gourds over most of the state; particularly large colonies can be seen at Brigantine NWR and at Cape May, where martins arrive in late March. One of the state's great wildlife spectacles is the August concentration of thousands of migrants in Cumberland County. The distinctive growling calls are rich, low, and throaty, a characteristic sound of summer in wet, open habitats.

Tubular body with long wings, large head and bill. Adult male glossy blue-black with darker wings.

Heavy body with long but broad wings; broad, shallowly notched tail. Female and young faintly mottled gray beneath with darker throat. Slow flight with much soaring.

Tree Swallow

Tachycineta bicolor

L 5.75" | **WS** 14.5" | **WT** 0.7 OZ (20 G)

The gleaming-bellied Tree Swallow is our most abundant and hardiest swallow, arriving in March and regularly lingering into December or even longer in mild winters. A cavity nester, this species is found in summer wherever old woodpecker holes or nest boxes are available; like all swallows, it prefers open, wet areas for feeding. Flocks of thousands are seen in August and September at Cape May and other coastal localities. The distinctive calls and song are high-pitched, metallic rippling trills and twitters.

parrow-sized, with pointed wings, small head and bill, and short, notched tail. Adults glistening green or blue above.

Short, fat body with rather short, broad wings and short, notched tail. Young birds dark sooty gray above. Flight weak and fluttering, with frequent short glides.

Northern Rough-winged Swallow

Stelgidopteryx serripennis

L 5.5″ | **WS** 14″ | **WT** 0.56 OZ (16 G)

Drab and less gregarious than other swallows, the Northern Rough-winged Swallow is a common but local summer resident wherever riverbanks and road cuts provide sites for individual pairs' nest burrows. Migrants are common in April and August in any open habitat, especially around ponds. Reliable locations for this species include Great Swamp NWR, Walkill NWR, and Worthington State Forest. Calls are low-pitched, relaxed, pleasant buzzes.

Broad, short wings and uniform plumage, dingy white on belly and tan-brown elsewhere. Flight easy and floating, with slow, regularly spaced wingbeats.

Bank Swallow

Riparia riparia

L 5.25″ | **WS** 13″ | **WT** 0.47 OZ (13.5 G)

The tiny size of the dashing Bank Swallow can be striking in the field, whether in mixed swallow flocks or at its breeding colonies in sandpits and steep river banks. Overall an uncommon bird, the Bank Swallow arrives in April and departs in September; migrants can be seen anywhere in the state, especially near water, but nesting birds tend to stay close to their dense colonies, which shift location from year to year as banks collapse or quarrying operations are resumed. Unlike the easy floating of Rough-winged Swallows and the labored flutters of Tree Swallows, the flight of the Bank Swallow is fast and direct. The distinctive call is a high-pitched, fast, electric-buzzer *trrzt-trrzt*.

Very small, with fast, strong flight. Wings noticeably darker than sandy brown back.

Very small and neatly marked. Short, deeply notched tail. Dark breast band contrasts with white throat, which curls up behind ear patch.

Cliff Swallow

Petrochelidon pyrrhonota

L 5.5″ | **WS** 13.5″ | **WT** 0.74 OZ (21 G)

The dark-plumaged, broad-winged Cliff Swallow is an uncommon migrant and scarce and declining breeding species, breeding where bridges, dams, and barns provide sites for its small colonies of jug-shaped mud nests. Nesting birds can be found at Bull's Island and on farms in northwestern New Jersey; migrants occur in May and September wherever swallows congregate. This is a quiet bird for a swallow, the call a soft, buzzy or burping rattle.

Dark throat and crown contrast with bright "headlight" on forehead and dull buffy breast.

Bulky body, large head; wide, blunt wings and short, squared tail. Dark throat, crown, and back contrast with pale buffy collar and rump.

Barn Swallow

Hirundo rustica

L 6.75″ | **WS** 15″ | **WT** 0.67 OZ (19 G)

Elegant and familiar, the long-winged, long-tailed Barn Swallow breeds throughout New Jersey wherever bridges and buildings provide sites for its open mud nest. Breeders and migrants are easily found from April to October in any open habitat; a few may linger into mild winters at Cape May. The loud, cheerful calls include an upslurred, nasal *hveet-hveet* and a panicked *hvip* given on the appearance of a predator; the song, often given from a perch on a wire or post, is a long, complex series of high-pitched trills and nasal notes.

Small, with small, round head and deeply forked tail, longest in adult male. Glossy blue-black above, yellowish buff below with dark throat.

Long, sharply pointed wings and deeply forked tail with white spots. Flight fast and elegant, wings drawn back with each deep beat.

Black-capped Chickadee

Poecile atricapilla

L 5.25″　|　**WS** 8″　|　**WT** 0.39 OZ (11 G)

Neatly plumaged black and gray, Black-capped Chickadees are common residents of forests and wooded suburbs, where they often nest in birdhouses and become habitual and confiding visitors to feeders, gorging themselves on suet and sunflower seeds. Breeding north of a line from southern Hunterdon County to the mouth of the Raritan River, in some years this species moves unpredictably into central and southern New Jersey in winter. Common calls include a fairly slow, raspy *chicka-dee-dee-dee*; the song is a slow, mellow, whistled *FEE-bee* or *FEE-bee-bee*.

Small, with long tail, big head. Inner wing and "shoulder" frosted white in fresh plumage; black bib sometimes smudgy or jagged where it meets breast.

Carolina Chickadee

Poecile carolinensis

L 4.75″ | **WS** 7.5″ | **WT** 0.37 OZ (10.5 G)

A common resident south of Hunterdon County and Raritan Bay, the Carolina Chickadee shares the habits of its northern relative, with which it overlaps in a narrow band. Identification can be difficult, and is compounded by the presence of hybrids and intergrades with intermediate appearance. The classic "chickadee" call of this species is slightly faster than that of the Black-capped; the typical song is higher-pitched and faster, a four-noted *FEE-bee-fee-bay*. Apparent hybrids in central New Jersey sing a slurred *FEEee-FEEay*.

ery small, with relatively short tail,
nall head. Entire wing dull dark
ray in fresh plumage; black bib
eets breast in neat, straight line.

Tufted Titmouse

Baeolophus bicolor

L 6.5″ | **WS** 9.75″ | **WT** 0.75 OZ (21.5 G)

The subtly beautiful, noisy Tufted Titmouse is common in wooded habitats throughout New Jersey; like its smaller relatives the chickadees, it is a familiar visitor to suburban yards and feeders. The chickadee-like calls are low-pitched, hoarse, and whining; the song, given as early as January, is a bright, low-pitched, whistled chant *PEET-a-PEET-a*, a characteristic sound of spring woodlands.

Sparrow-sized, with long tail and large, crested head. Dove-gray above, paler below, with peach wash on sides.

Black forehead and large staring black eye.

Brown Creeper

Certhia americana

L 5.25″ | **WS** 7.75″ | **WT** 0.29 OZ (8.4 G)

Tiny, common, and easily overlooked, the bark-colored Brown Creeper is a winter resident of forested habitats throughout the state; a few breed at High Point State Park and Stokes State Forest and along the Delaware River. Creepers flock with chickadees and nuthatches, climbing quietly up trunks and branches, then flying to the base of a nearby tree to begin a new ascent. The call is a long, thin, hissing *seeee*; the song, conspicuous in quiet woods in early spring, is a measured whistle *trees-trees-I-love-trees*.

ny, with very long tail and
in, down-curved bill.
ull to bright white below,
omplexly patterned
ray, black, and buff above.
reamy wing stripe
onspicuous in flight.

White-breasted Nuthatch

Sitta carolinensis

L 5.75″ | **WS** 11″ | **WT** 0.74 OZ (21 G)

Clad in the dapper plumage of a tiny tuxedoed penguin, the stubby, big-billed White-breasted Nuthatch is a common resident of forests, wooded parks, and suburbs throughout the state, often flocking at feeders with chickadees and titmouses. Nuthatches are active and noisy, hitching industriously up tree trunks like tiny woodpeckers, then creeping back down head-first. The call is a hoarse, nasal honking *ANK-ANK*, given in a long, faster series as a song.

Sparrow-sized, with short, broad tail, big head, dagger-like bill. White face, blackish cap, dull orange on undertail and flank.

Red-breasted Nuthatch

Sitta canadensis

L 4.5″ | **WS** 8.5″ | **WT** 0.35 OZ (10 G)

The small, dainty, colorful Red-breasted Nuthatch is an
irregular fall and winter visitor across New Jersey, favoring
dark, especially coniferous, woods. It often flocks with
other woodland species at bird feeders. In years of abundance,
migrants of this species arrive as early as August, and a
few may remain to breed the following spring. Just as acrobatic
as its larger, more flamboyant relative, the Red-breasted is
less conspicuous, with quieter, thinner, higher-pitched
calls *eeng-eeng.*

Chickadee-sized, with
short, narrow tail, big
head, short bill. Black
line through eye,
white line above. Entire
breast and belly dull
rusty orange.

Winter Wren

Troglodytes hiemalis

L 4"　|　**WS** 5.5"　|　**WT** 0.32 OZ (9 G)

One of our smallest songbirds, the dark, stub-tailed Winter Wren is an inconspicuous and uncommon migrant and winter resident across New Jersey; a few breed in dark, wet woodlands at High Point, Stokes State Forest, and elsewhere in the Northwest. Migration is concentrated in April and October, when birds frequent the damp ground beneath thickets and along small forest streams. The common call is a loud, husky *cheb-cheb*, the song a high-pitched series of fast trills.

Tiny, with short, often cocked tail; short, finely dotted wings; short bill. Dark brown above, with pale eye stripe.

Breast vaguely spotted or scalloped, flank neatly barred black. Often bobs up and down on bent legs.

House Wren

Troglodytes aedon

L 4.75″ │ **WS** 6″ │ **WT** 0.39 OZ (11 G)

The small, plain House Wren is easily found at High Point, Great Swamp NWR, Brigantine NWR, and throughout the state wherever nest boxes or woodpecker holes provide nesting sites. Arriving in April and departing in October, House Wrens feed inconspicuously in thickets, but mount conspicuous perches to sing their long series of dry trills at different pitches. Calls are toneless and rasping.

Small, with long, often cocked tail; short, finely barred wings; slightly curved bill. Dull brown above.

Plain face and underparts. Singing birds hold tail down and point yellow-based bill skyward.

Birdhouse Birds

Many cavity-nesting species—from owls and woodpeckers to chickadees and bluebirds—will accept birdhouses for roosting and breeding. Construction plans are readily available, but the most important consideration is the placement of the box: Tree Swallows, for example, prefer open fields, while Wood Duck houses should be hung over forrested ponds. Wrens are some of the most eager inhabitants of man-made cavities, and even the most primitive box will attract House or Carolina Wrens over most of New Jersey. Not all wren nests will fledge young, however; these birds are well known for constructing multiple nests in their territories, only one of which is used for egg-laying and the rearing of young.

Carolina Wren

Thryothorus ludovicianus

L 5.5" | **WS** 7.5" | **WT** 0.74 OZ (21 G)

Our largest and most colorful wren, the Carolina Wren is a resident of tangled thickets throughout New Jersey; most abundant in the South, it may be subject to occasional die-offs in the Northwest during hard winters. Sometimes difficult to see in the dense foliage they prefer, Carolina Wrens also visit feeders for suet and seeds. The wide range of calls includes a ringing, wooden *tick-tick* and a squirrel-like rattle; the bright, loud song is a rolling chant *TKEE-tee-tee TKEE-tee-tee*.

Sparrow-sized, with long, often cocked tail.

White below with dull orange wash. Singing birds hold tail down and point open bill skyward.

Short, white-spotted wings; long, curved bill. Rich brown above. Bright white eye stripe.

Marsh Wren

Cistothorus palustris

L 5″ | **WS** 6″ | **WT** 0.39 OZ (11 G)

The sturdy, heavily marked Marsh Wren sings its squeaky, gurgling trills from fresh and brackish marshes across New Jersey, usually invisible deep in the cattails or reeds. From May to September, patient observers can see breeders in the Meadowlands, at Great Swamp and Brigantine NWR, and in the freshwater marshes of Sussex County; migrants occur in dry, brushy habitat, and a few birds winter on the coast. Calls include a sharp, dry chip resembling that of a yellowthroat.

Sparrow-sized, with medium-long, often cocked tail; short, barred wings; long bill.

Often hidden deep in aquatic vegetation. Richly colored reddish-brown upperparts, streaked blackish back, dark crown.

Golden-crowned Kinglet

Regulus satrapa

L 4″ | **WS** 7″ | **WT** 0.21 OZ (6 G)

Our smallest songbird, the hyperactive, barely-there Golden-crowned Kinglet is a common migrant and fairly common winterer throughout the state; a few breed in dense conifers in the extreme Northwest. Migrants, most common in April and October, roam open woodlands with chickadees and creepers; numbers can be especially high in fall at Sandy Hook and Island Beach. The call, a rushed *see-see-see*, is very high-pitched and thin; the seldom heard song is an accelerating *see-see-see-a-deedeedee*.

Very small, with short tail, tiny bill. Underparts grayish white, crown bordered by black and white stripes.

Adult male with red center to crown; young and female with yellow crown. Gray upperparts contrast with greenish in wing.

Ruby-crowned Kinglet

Regulus calendula

L 4.25″ | **WS** 7.5″ | **WT** 0.23 OZ (6.5 G)

The chubby, short-tailed Ruby-crowned Kinglet is a common migrant throughout the state in early May and September, roaming open woodlands with chickadees and creepers; wintering birds are scarce most years except in the south. The low-pitched call is a stuttering *ch-dek*; the song, often heard on migration and even on warm winter days, is an astonishingly loud, musical *see-see-see-tee-DOOdala-DOOdala*.

Very small, with short tail, tiny bill. Underparts washed olive green, dull face with large white eye ring.

Adult male with red crown patch; young and female crown plain. Short tail, horizontal pose, constant activity distinguish from flycatchers.

Blue-gray Gnatcatcher

Polioptila caerulea

L 4.5″ | **WS** 6″ | **WT** 0.21 OZ (6 G)

Tiny, active, and very long-tailed, the Blue-gray Gnatcatcher is a common April and September migrant and fairly common breeder in forests throughout New Jersey. Favored sites include Garret Mountain, Great Swamp NWR, Brigantine NWR, and Belleplain State Forest. Gnatcatchers feed frantically among leafy twigs, high during the breeding season, lower on migration. Their calls include high, wheezy lisps, and the song is a vague, rambling series of scratchy tones and chips.

Very small; lean and long-tailed. Dove-gray above, white below, with bright white eye ring and long, sharp bill.

Long tail with white outer feathers constantly flipped and flirted. Adult male with fine black border to blue-gray crown.

Wood Thrush

Hylocichla mustelina

L 7.75″ | **WS** 13″ | **WT** 1.6 OZ (47 G)

Deep-voiced and colorful, the pudgy Wood Thrush breeds throughout New Jersey. Unlike the smaller brown thrushes, this species is rarely conspicuous as a migrant, and breeders simply appear on territory in late April, departing in September. Preferring old forests with dense undergrowth, nesting Wood Thrushes are easily found at Stokes State Forest, Mills Reservation, Princeton's Institute Woods, and other woodland sites. The call is a bubbling *pip-pip-pip*; the rich song is a slurred *eeolay* followed by a higher-pitched trill.

Size of a large, plump sparrow, with short tail, short wings, large dark eye. Rusty above, brightest on crown.

Bright white beneath, with large black spots reaching flank and belly. Often bounds robin-like across forest floor.

Hermit Thrush

Catharus guttatus

L 6.75″ | **WS** 11.5″ | **WT** 1.1 OZ (31 G)

The most common of our small brown thrushes and the only one at all likely to be seen in winter, the elegant little Hermit Thrush is also the easiest to identify, with its distinctive habit of slowly raising and lowering its fox-colored tail. Migrants occur in any wooded area in April and again from October to December; winterers are most abundant in the south, but can be found wherever the ground is snow-free and water open. A few breed at High Point, Stokes State Forest, and other northwestern sites; nesting also takes place infrequently in the Pine Barrens. This species' calls include a low-pitched, no-nonsense *tup*, a characteristic sound of late autumn woods; the famous song begins with a pure whistle, followed by an ethereal falsetto swirling.

Size of a large sparrow, with fairly short tail, short wings, large dark eye. Dull brown back and wings, warm reddish rump and tail.

Dull whitish breast with distinct black spots, narrow white eye ring; reddish tail slowly raised and lowered.

Tail often cocked

Gray-cheeked Thrush

Catharus minimus

L 7.25″ | **WS** 13″ | **WT** 1.1 OZ (32 G)

A very shy, cold gray-brown bird, the Gray-cheeked Thrush is an uncommon migrant in May and September, with some birds lingering into late October. Most often detected by its harsh, down-slurred call *verr*, it can be seen by the quiet observer at Garret Mountain, Rifle Camp Park, Princeton's Institute Woods, and other forested localities throughout the state. Spring birds may sing a buzzy, gargling song that falls, rises, and falls at the end. The lookalike Bicknell's Thrush, smaller and more warmly colored, is a scarce migrant at the same sites.

Size of a large sparrow, with fairly short tail, short wings, large dark eye. Uniformly dull gray-brown above, distinct black spots on breast, narrow white eye ring.

Swainson's Thrush

Catharus ustulatus

L 7″ | **WS** 12″ | **WT** 1.1 OZ (31 G)

The brown, bright-faced Swainson's Thrush is a common migrant throughout the state in May and September, when it can be seen in most wooded habitats, including treed suburbs. Like all the brown thrushes, this species is most often seen feeding quietly on the ground in shady forests. Garret Mountain, Rifle Camp Park, and Princeton's Institute Woods are usually reliable sites. Often quite vocal, migrants give a hollow, liquid *plink*, like a drop of water striking a metal bowl. Spring birds sing a rising, choking song *vreea-vreea-VREEP*.

Size of a large sparrow, with fairly short tail, short wings, large dark eye. Uniformly dull brown above, distinct black spots on yellow-tinged breast, broad yellowish eye ring.

Veery
Catharus fuscescens
L 7″ | **WS** 12″ | **WT** 1.1 OZ (31 G)

The Veery is a shy woodland thrush, better known for its oddly beautiful song than for its subtly fox-colored plumage. A common breeder in forest understory in the northern half of the state and the Pine Barrens, this species is also a common migrant in May and September over the entire state. Summering birds can be heard and seen at High Point, Stokes State Forest, and Great Swamp NWR. The frequent call is a harsh, abruptly down-slurred *VEEer*; the song is a metallic descending spiral *VEER-veer-veer-veery*.

Size of a large sparrow, with fairly short tail, short wings, large dark eye. Uniformly soft rusty brown above.

Pale grayish white beneath, with faint, diffuse spotting across yellow-tinged breast.

Brown Thrushes

Furtive shade dwellers, the "spotted" thrushes (pages 207–212) can be very challenging, slipping silently away into the foliage after giving the most fleeting of glimpses. While the color and pattern of the upperparts are important characters, they can be hard to determine in the dark habitats these birds prefer. From below, the faint cinnamon dotting of a Veery's (below left) breast identifies it immediately; the large, round black spots of a Wood Thrush (below right, top) are equally diagnostic. Wood Thrushes also have thick, bright eye rings; most Swainson's Thrushes (below right, bottom) show clearly yellowish eye rings and spectacles. The most distinctive behavior in this group is the slow raising and lowering of the Hermit Thrush's tail, allowing that species to be identified even in dimmest silhouette.

American Robin
Turdus migratorius

L 10″ | **WS** 17″ | **WT** 2.7 OZ (77 G)

Perhaps New Jersey's most familiar songbird, the large, boisterous American Robin is a familiar warm-season sight on lawns and woodland edges; large numbers also winter most years, spending most of their time in wet woodlands where they feed on berries, often in mixed flocks with waxwings and bluebirds. When feeding on the ground, robins run, then abruptly stop, cocking their head, drooping their wings, and lifting the tail. The northward flight begins in late winter; the spectacular autumn migration can bring hundreds of thousands to Cape May in October. The loud calls include a melodious chuckle, a thin *seee*, and a nervous, insistent *peek peek*. The song, often given well before dawn in spring, is a hoarse but cheerful carol *churee churew churee churew*.

Juvenile with patchy orange and white breast, black spotting.

Large and fairly long-tailed, with full breast and small head. Olive brown above, female with dull orange breast.

Broken eye ring, black and white streaked throat. Adult male with blackish head.

Eastern Bluebird

Sialia sialis

L 7″ | **WS** 13″ | **WT** 1.1 OZ (31 G)

The round-shouldered, pot-bellied Eastern Bluebird is a common resident of open habitats across the state, breeding in abandoned woodpecker holes and competing with Tree Swallows for nest boxes. Look for this species on farm fields and woodland edges at Great Swamp NWR, Brigantine NWR, and Cape May. Many birds overwinter in mild years, often associating loosely with robins, waxwings, and other fruit-eaters at berry-laden trees and bushes. Migrants are especially conspicuous in October, when small flocks pass overhead with sweet, descending whistles *purwee*; the gently fluttering, swooping flight is distinctive, with short tails, small heads, and rounded wings giving the birds a blocky appearance. The song is a soft, harsh warble given from a low tree or wire.

Often perches with bill down and shoulders hunched. Adult male glistening blue with red breast and neck sides.

ze of large sparrow,
th short tail, long
ng, round head.
dult female browner
 head and back.

Very young birds
neatly spotted above
and below, but shape
and blue in wings
and tail distinctive.

Gray Catbird

Dumetella carolinensis

L 8.5″ | **WS** 11″ | **WT** 1.3 OZ (37 G)

The slender, somberly plumaged Gray Catbird is an abundant migrant and summer resident in overgrown fields and on tangled woodland edges throughout New Jersey; a few winter in the south, but most arrive in late April and depart in September. Often secretive, catbirds are most easily seen in late summer when they gorge themselves on wild grapes, berries, and poison ivy fruits. The distinctive calls include a whining, cat-like *meew* and a crackling *ack-ack*; the song is a long, squeaky warble.

Smaller, slenderer than robin; long tail, short, rounded wings, small head. Bluish-slate all over with neat black cap.

Deep chestnut undertail contrasts with blackish tail.

Northern Mockingbird

Mimus polyglottos

L 10″ | **WS** 14″ | **WT** 1.7 OZ (49 G)

Noisy and assertive, the sleek, neatly patterned Northern Mockingbird is a common resident throughout New Jersey in old fields, suburbs, and even city centers. Notorious for its nighttime singing, this species is often seen perched on wires or at the top of fruit-bearing trees and bushes, where it chases off all intruders. The call is a loud, low-pitched *chack*, the loud song an almost endless series of repeated phrases mimicking other birds, domestic animals, and even mechanical noises.

Smaller, slenderer than robin. Long tail and short, rounded wings with large white patches conspicuous in flight. Adult with dull yellow eye.

Juvenile faintly spotted beneath. At all ages, often feeds on ground with wings half-spread.

Brown Thrasher

Toxostoma rufum

L 11.5″ | **WS** 13″ | **WT** 2.4 OZ (69 G)

The colorful and noisy Brown Thrasher is an uncommon breeding bird in overgrown fields throughout New Jersey, generally arriving in April and departing in September; a few scattered individuals overwinter, especially in the south. This declining species can still be found reliably at Brigantine NWR, Assunpink, and Cape May; the highest densities are in the Pine Barrens. Thrashers sing their loud, distinctly phrased songs from wires and dead trees: *rocket-rocket, twee-twee, ratchet-ratchet*. The call is a dry *chekt*.

Lanky and long-tailed, with short wings and sickle-shaped bill. Foxy red above with gray face, white wingbars, neat black spots and streaks below.

Digs and scratches noisily in leaves and twigs. Flight awkward and fluttering, with choppy wingbeat.

American Pipit

Anthus rubescens

L 6.5″ | **WS** 10.5″ | **WT** 0.74 OZ (21 G)

The classic "invisible bird," the unassuming American
Pipit is almost never seen unless it is first heard giving its
inconspicuous two-noted call *pss-psit* high overhead. Careful
scanning in April and, especially, October may reveal small
flocks of these sturdy, long-legged brown birds walking in
straight lines across fields, dry lakeshores, and beaches; the
long, square tail is frequently bobbed. Liberty Sod Farm, Sandy
Hook, Island Beach, and Barnegat Light are good places to look
and listen for this fairly common migrant.

Plain olive-brown above,
with long, square tail
and sturdy dark legs.
White outer tail feathers
are conspicuous in
strong, swooping flight.

Feeds on bare ground, walking
purposefully and frequently
bobbing tail. Fall and winter birds
heavily marked below.

European Starling

Sturnus vulgaris

L 8.5" | **WS** 16" | **WT** 2.9 OZ (82 G) | ♂ > ♀

Introduced from Europe in the late nineteenth century, the aggressive and stunningly beautiful European Starling is now one of New Jersey's most common birds, found in every habitat wherever natural holes, nest boxes, or buildings offer nest sites; pairs often evict, and sometimes even kill, other cavity nesters such as bluebirds and woodpeckers. Large flocks waddle methodically over lawns and fields at any season, and huge, messy, noisy winter roosts can form in cities and suburbs. Flying birds easily identified by deep-bellied body; short, triangular, translucent brown wings; and stubby tail. Gifted mimics, starlings sing a long, irregular series of phrases, sweetly musical and harshly grating; juveniles give a raspy *shrkk* in flight.

Fist-sized and rotund, with sharply pointed "stuck-on" bill and very short tail. Winter birds with dense white spotting on green-black underparts.

Breeding adult glossy
black with brown-tinged
wings, yellow bill.
Male with blue bill base,
female with pink.

Juveniles mouse-brown
with white throat,
short dark bill. Spotted
winter plumage
comes in gradually and
patchwise.

Cedar Waxwing

Bombycilla cedrorum

L 7.25" | **WS** 12" | **WT** 1.1 OZ (32 G)

The elegant and delicately colored Cedar Waxwing is a
common but somewhat irregular resident across New Jersey,
most familiar in the fall and winter flocks that descend on
woodlands, suburbs, and even parking lots to strip trees and
bushes of their fruit. Wintering birds are often found with
bluebirds or robins. Large numbers migrate through the state
in May and September, especially along the coast, and breeders
can be found unpredictably in any woodland. At any season,
waxwings are most easily detected by their high, lisping calls.
Birds overhead resemble small starlings with their triangular
wings and short necks, but the stubby tail is conspicuously
tipped yellow.

Sleek and short-tailed,
with crested, short-
billed "hammerhead."
Yellow-tipped gray
tail contrasts with
fawn-colored back and
breast; variable red
tips on wing feathers.

Young birds less neatly masked, with diffuse brown streaking below.

Ovenbird

Seiurus aurocapilla

L 6″ | **WS** 9.5″ | **WT** 0.68 OZ (19.5 G)

The famous ringing crescendo *teacher-teacher-TEACHer* of the drab, ground-dwelling Ovenbird is conspicuous in mid-summer in old forests throughout the state. This common species is easily found at Stokes State Forest, Belleplain State Forest, and Brigantine NWR, walking quietly mid-wood through the leaf litter or singing from a low branch just above the forest understory. Migrants pass through in large numbers in April and again in August and September, using habitats from forest to urban parks.

Sparrow-sized, plump and short-tailed. Dull green-brown above, neatly striped black on white below.

Sings from ground or low branch. Bright white eye ring on bland face; orange crown patch often inconspicuous.

Worm-eating Warbler

Helmitheros vermivorum

L 5.25″ | **WS** 8.5″ | **WT** 0.46 OZ (13 G)

A sluggish brown warbler of deciduous woods, the Worm-eating Warbler is a fairly common breeding bird of northwestern and southern New Jersey; it can be found from late April to August on well-treed slopes or in wet woodlands in Stokes, Worthington, and Belleplain State Forests, where it feeds quietly in dense clusters of dry leaves or in low brush. Migrants can occur anywhere in the state in early September, but are quiet and often reclusive. Breeding birds can be located by listening for their distinctive song, a dry trill on a single pitch similar to but faster and buzzier than the song of a Chipping Sparrow or Pine Warbler. The common call is a harsh, penetrating *tsick*.

Sparrow-sized, short-tailed and spike-billed. Green-brown above, whitish undertail with short black streaks, head boldly striped black.

Louisiana Waterthrush

Parkesia motacilla

L 6″ | **WS** 10″ | **WT** 0.72 OZ (20.5 G)

One of the first warblers to return in spring and to depart in fall, the uncommon Louisiana Waterthrush is a local breeder along small wooded streams over most of the state. Look and listen for this brown, ground-dwelling bird from late March to early August at Stokes State Forest, the New Jersey Brigade Area, and Belleplain. This species walks deliberately on bright pink legs through dry leaves or shallow water, slowly bobbing its tail. The call is a flat metallic *chup,* the song loud, clear whistles followed by a hurried series of chips.

Sparrow-sized, short-tailed and heavy-billed. Brown above, blurry streaks on breast; throat white, flank vaguely buffy. Strong white eye line.

Northern Waterthrush

Parkesia noveboracensis

L 6″ | **WS** 9.5″ | **WT** 0.63 OZ (18 G)

The Northern Waterthrush is a common migrant throughout
the state and a scarce breeding bird in boggy woods at High
Point, Stokes State Forest, and other forested northwestern
sites. Migrants occur in damp habitats in May and from July to
September, walking deliberately on dull pinkish legs through
dry leaves or shallow water, bobbing their tails rather quickly.
The call is a loud, sharp, cardinal-like *teek*, the low-pitched
song a series of measured phrases at different pitches *chur-chur
chip-chip chup-chup-chup.*

parrow-sized,
hort-tailed and fairly
hort-billed. Brown
bove, neat black
treaks on whitish or
ull yellowish breast
nd throat. Narrow
ellowish or whitish
ye line.

Golden-winged Warbler

Vermivora chrysoptera

L 4.75″ | **WS** 7.5″ | **WT** 0.31 OZ (8.8 G)

Now very scarce anywhere in its range, the tiny, acrobatic Golden-winged Warbler is a rare migrant throughout the state and a very rare breeding bird in brushy fields and overgrown powerline cuts in northwestern New Jersey. A few are still seen in May and September at such migration hotspots as Garret Mountain, Palmyra, and, especially, Cape May. Reforestation and interbreeding with the more abundant Blue-winged Warbler threaten this species' survival. The song—also given by intergrades—is a fast, buzzy *bee-bzz-bzz-bzz*.

Very small and delicate, with short tail. Apparently "pure" birds with large yellow wing patch, gray or black throat and broad mask.

Adult male chickadee-like, with yellow crown. Yellowish on breast and faint break in wing patch probably signs of interbreeding with Blue-winged Warbler.

Blue-winged Warbler
Vermivora cyanoptera

L 4.75″ | **WS** 7.5″ | **WT** 0.3 OZ (8.5 G)

A common migrant and fairly common breeder, especially in the south, the bright yellow Blue-winged Warbler can be heard and seen from May to September in overgrown fields and thickets throughout the state. Migrants are reliably seen at such migration hotspots as Garret Mountain, Palmyra, and Cape May. This bird commonly interbreeds with the much less common Golden-winged Warbler, producing young that combine the plumage features of both parents. The song—also given by intergrades—is a slow, uncouth, falling, two-noted buzz *BEE-brrzz*.

Bright lemon yellow with bluish wings, white wingbars, neat black eye line. Spread tail shows large white spots.

Yellow in wingbars and dusky head patterning probably signs of interbreeding with Golden-winged Warbler.

Black-and-white Warbler

Mniotilta varia

L 5.25″ | **WS** 8.25″ | **WT** 0.37 OZ (10.7 G)

The neatly striped Black-and-white Warbler is one of our
most common migrant warblers, ubiquitous in deciduous
woods in April and September; breeding birds can be found
at High Point, Great Swamp, Belleplain, and in nearly
any moderately extensive forest in the state. This species feeds
by creeping busily along trunks and large limbs, recalling
a small, hyperactive, black and white nuthatch. The easily
recognized song is a slightly wheezing chant *WEE-see-WEE-see*
like a distant squeaky wheel.

Fairly small and
short-tailed, with dark
crown and coarsely
streaked and spotted
undertail. Creeps
acrobatically along
trunks and branches.

Boldly striped head
and underparts,
streaked gray and
black above. Adult
male with black chin.

Prothonotary Warbler

Protonotaria citrea

L 5.5″ | **WS** 8.75″ | **WT** 0.56 OZ (16 G)

A golden bird with a golden voice, the stocky, short-tailed Prothonotary Warbler is an uncommon breeding bird of southern swamps and a fairly scarce migrant across the state. Look for it from April to August at Belleplain and Glassboro Woods, where it nests—uniquely among New Jersey's warblers—in woodpecker holes and nest boxes low over the water of wooded ponds. The call note is a rich, round chip, the song a loud, unvaried, but full and pleasing *sweep-sweep-sweep*.

Sparrow-sized. Short-tailed and front-heavy, with full belly and long, spike-like bill. Gray wings contrast with yellow head. Female duller overall with gray-green crown and back.

Conspicuous white tail spots from below or in flight; large black eye on plain face. Adult male bright golden.

Tennessee Warbler

Oreothlypis peregrina

L 4.75″ | **WS** 7.75″ | **WT** 0.35 OZ (10 G)

The long-winged, short-tailed Tennessee Warbler is an uncommon September migrant across New Jersey; it is usually much scarcer on the northbound journey in May. Garret Mountain, Palmyra, and Cape May are good places to look for this species, which feeds high in the treetops in spring but often descends to eye level in fall. The song, infrequently heard in New Jersey, is a three-parted mechanical rattle *tick-tick teeka-teeka trrrtrrr*; the call is a sharp, incisive *tseek*.

Rather small; short-tailed and long-winged. White undertail, broad pale eye stripe. Female and young green-yellow beneath.

Spring male grass-green above, with bluish crown and broad pale eye stripe.

Orange-crowned Warbler

Oreothlypis celata

L 5″ | **WS** 7.25″ | **WT** 0.32 OZ (9 G)

The short-winged, long-tailed (and poorly named) Orange-crowned Warbler is a scarce October migrant and a rare winterer; this is one of our rarest spring warblers. Fond of goldenrod and ragweed, it is most often found feeding close to the ground on cold autumn days at Sandy Hook, Island Beach, and Cape May, or, less often, on weedy fields inland. Wintering birds can occur anywhere in the state in brushy fields and at woodland edges. The sparrow-like call is a lisping *tsip*.

Rather small; long-tailed and short-winged. Yellow undertail, narrow eye ring broken by fine black eye line. Breast with faint blurry streaks.

Uniformly dingy greenish-yellow above and below, with slightly contrasting gray tone to head; orange crown almost never seen. Fine black eye line creates severe facial expression.

Nashville Warbler

Oreothlypis ruficapilla

L 4.75″ | **WS** 7.5″ | **WT** 0.3 OZ (8.7 G)

Small and slight, the active, brightly colored Nashville Warbler is a fairly common May and September migrant throughout New Jersey; a very few linger to breed in bogs at High Point and other northwestern sites. Migrants can be found at Garret Mountain, Palmyra, Cape May, and anywhere warblers congregate; they feed at all heights, from treetops to eye level, and occasionally wag the tail. The call is a thin, high, sparrow-like *tsip*, the song a two-parted *psit-psit dededede*.

Rather small, fairly long-tailed. Clear yellow undertail contrasts with white belly; yellow breast, blue sides of head.

Clear white eye ring, bright yellow throat. Smaller, slenderer, with thinner legs and bill than vireos or larger warblers.

Mourning Warbler

Geothlypis philadelphia

L 5.25" | **WS** 7.5" | **WT** 0.44 OZ (12.5 G)

Sluggish and reclusive, the dull-colored Mourning Warbler is an uncommon migrant across the state in late May and August, when it can be found hopping (unlike the walking gait of Connecticut Warbler) inconspicuously through low streamside vegetation at Garret Mountain or Palmyra; it seems to prefer coastal sites, such as Sandy Hook and Cape May, in autumn. Spring migrants often sing, a rich, low-pitched *churr-churr churry-churry*; fall migrants are quiet, occasionally giving a low, flat chip note.

Medium-sized, with short tail and fairly long yellowish undertail. Gray hood with gray or dull yellow throat; may have thin, broken eye ring.

Spring adult with black smudge on breast, black between eye and short, thick bill.

Common Yellowthroat
Geothlypis trichas

L 5" | **WS** 6.75" | **WT** 0.35 OZ (10 G)

The brightly colored and inquisitive Common Yellowthroat is a common breeding bird in wet thickets, overgrown fields, and densely vegetated salt and freshwater marshes; migrants can appear in any habitat in April and from August to October. A few may winter in southern coastal marshes. Hard to miss in season and in habitat anywhere in the state, this species feeds low in thick vegetation and is most easily detected by its loud, smacking call and musical, caroling song *WICH-ery-WICH-ery*.

Medium-small, pot-bellied, with short yellowish undertail. Breast and throat yellow, sides of head dusky gray.

Short bill, medium-long tail. Adult male with broad velvety mask separated from crown by silver-gray band.

Connecticut Warbler

Oporornis agilis

L 5.75″ | **WS** 9″ | **WT** 0.53 OZ (15 G)

Large and short-tailed, the phlegmatic, somberly colored
Connecticut Warbler is a scarce September migrant along the
coast; one of New Jersey's least common and thus most sought-
after warblers, it is often confused with the Nashville Warbler
and the Common Yellowthroat, both of which are smaller,
longer-tailed, and more given to feeding in the open. Migrants
are most often seen at Sandy Hook and Cape May; they are
found low in dense vegetation, walking deliberately as they
feed. The call is a soft, dull *dip*.

Large for a warbler; stocky,
with short tail and long yellowish
undertail. Throat dull gray or
whitish. Adults with clear gray head,
browner in young. Bright, thin
eye ring. Stout bill, short tail.

Kentucky Warbler

Geothlypis formosa

L 5.25″ | **WS** 8.5″ | **WT** 0.49 OZ (14 G)

The handsome, ground-dwelling Kentucky Warbler is an uncommon and local breeding bird in moist woods in the southern half of New Jersey. It can be found feeding on or near the ground from May to August in thick forest understory at Glassboro Woods, Belleplain, and damp woodlands in Cumberland County; it is much less common in the north, but can be looked for at Scherman Hoffman and the New Jersey Brigade Area. The distinctive song is a rollicking *chuy-chuy-chuy,* given from a low, often invisible perch.

Medium-sized and portly, with short tail. Bright yellow beneath, with olive upperparts and yellow spectacle setting off dark crown and moustache.

Yellow-breasted Chat

Icteria virens

L 7.5″ | **WS** 9.75″ | **WT** 0.88 OZ (25 G)

Our largest warbler, the noisy but skulking Yellow-breasted Chat is a fairly common summer resident of tangled thickets in southern New Jersey; it is a scarce migrant and breeder in the northern half of the state. From April to September, it screeches and yowls, often unseen, at Cape May and in overgrown fields in Cumberland and Salem Counties, where a few overwinter each year. The remarkable song is a long series of variable clucks, whistles, and yelps, sometimes given in an exaggeratedly slow flight display with dangling legs.

Size of a large sparrow, with very long tail and thick, arched bill. Bright yellow breast and clean white belly. Short dark mask outlined white above and below.

American Redstart

Setophaga ruticilla

L 5.25″ | **WS** 7.75″ | **WT** 0.29 OZ (8.3 G)

The spectacular American Redstart is one of our most abundant migrant warblers, found in any woodland habitat throughout the state in May and in August and September; a common nester in northern New Jersey's forests, it is less widespread as a breeder in the south. Redstarts are as conspicuous for their ostentatious behavior as they are for their bright plumage, constantly hopping and flitting through the foliage, often at eye level, while spreading their showy, butterfly-like wings and tail. Migrants associate with vireos, flycatchers, and other warblers, and are often the most abundant species in the flock. The extremely variable songs include an emphatic, hissing *see-see-see-SEE* and a thin, chanting *seeya-seeya-seeya*; the common call is a bright, sweet chip.

Small. Long, broad tail often spread. Slender body and short, flat bill. Young male with black flecks on head and breast.

Female soft dove-gray with bright yellow at base of tail, in wing, and on breast side.

Very energetic when feeding, flitting and darting into the air to take insects. Adult male black and orange.

Northern Parula

Setophaga americana

L 4.5″ | **WS** 7″ | **WT** 0.3 OZ (8.6 G)

The tiny, short-tailed Northern Parula is a common and colorful migrant statewide in May and throughout the autumn, with smaller numbers remaining to breed at scattered locations throughout New Jersey; migrants are found wherever warblers concentrate, while nesting birds can be looked for at Worthington State Forest, Great Swamp NWR, and in the Pine Barrens. The variable songs include a series of grumbling buzzes and a brilliant ascending run *brrrzzz-ZZP.*

White eye crescents; short, pale-based bill. Adult male with black and rusty band below throat.

Very small, with short tail, round body, and round head. White wingbars, yellow throat and breast sharply cut off from white belly.

Canada Warbler
Cardellina canadensis

L 5.25" | **WS** 8" | **WT** 0.36 OZ (10.3 G)

Long-tailed and neatly patterned, the bluish-backed Canada
Warbler is a common migrant in August and September and
a fairly common visitor in May; drastically decreasing as a
breeder, a few still nest at High Point, in Stokes State Forest,
and at other damp wooded sites in the extreme northwest.
Migrants are found at Garret Mountain, Great Swamp NWR,
and Palmyra, among other sites. The call is a distinctive sharp
tzip, the song a chatter followed by yellowthroat-like phrases
tippa-tippa-wichery.

Small, with long tail.
Neat, unmarked dark
gray on wing and
back; lemon below, with
yellow spectacle.

Large, round head and
short bill. Generally
low in trees and damp
thickets. Adult male
with black surrounding
bright yellow throat.

Wilson's Warbler

Cardellina pusilla

L 4.75″ | **WS** 7″ | **WT** 0.27 OZ (7.7 G)

Nervous, active, and uncommon, the long-tailed, brightly colored Wilson's Warbler migrates in small numbers across the state in May and September. This species is not guaranteed anywhere in the state, but can be looked for feeding busily in low trees and bushes at Garret Mountain, Princeton, Palmyra, and Cape May. The call is a distinctive squeaky *chiv*; the variable song, sometimes heard on spring migration, is a loose, rattling trill.

Small, pudgy, and long-tailed. Golden underparts contrast with unspotted dull slaty tail; broad golden stripe above eye, darker crown.

Often cocks and twitches tail. Adult male with round black crown patch.

Hooded Warbler

Setophaga citrina

L 5.25″ | **WS** 7″ | **WT** 0.37 OZ (10.5 G)

The long-tailed, woods-loving Hooded Warbler is a common but often reclusive breeder across New Jersey. Present from April to September, it sings from low perches in deciduous forest at Worthington State Forest, the New Jersey Brigade Area, and Belleplain; migrants are seen in small numbers at Garret Mountain, Palmyra, and Cape May. Like many other deep-woods warblers, this species is most easily detected by its call note, a loud, sweet *chap*, and its emphatic song *weech-weech-weeCHOa*.

Medium-sized, with long, expressive tail and large bill. Golden face set off against green shoulder and dark cap.

Large white spots visible when tail is flipped and spread. Adult male's golden face and forehead surrounded by inky black hood.

Yellow Warbler

Setophaga petechia

L 5″ | **WS** 8″ | **WT** 0.33 OZ (9.5 G)

Fairly large, chunky, and tame, the aptly named Yellow Warbler is a common migrant and breeding bird at marshland edges and in damp willow thickets throughout New Jersey. Migrants are easily found flocking with other warblers at Garret Mountain, Belleplain, Cape May, and even urban parks; spring birds arrive in mid-April, and the southward passage begins as early as July, with most individuals already gone by September. Breeding birds are widespread, but most abundant in wet habitats such as Great Swamp NWR, the Meadowlands, or Brigantine NWR, where they avoid large trees in favor of shrubby willows and dogwoods. The call is loud and sweet, the familiar song a bright, well-cadenced *seet-seet-seetseetSEET*.

Chunky, with long wing and notably short tail. Yellow edges on wing feathers, neat pale yellow eye ring on blank yellow face.

Underside of tail mostly yellow. Adult male irregularly streaked reddish below.

Some young birds in fall drab, but short, yellow-spotted tail, yellow-edged wings, and neat pale eye ring identify them.

Chestnut-sided Warbler

Setophaga pensylvanica

L 5″ | **WS** 7.75″ | **WT** 0.34 OZ (9.6 G)

Small and active, the neat green and white Chestnut-sided Warbler is a common migrant in May and August throughout New Jersey and an uncommon breeding bird in roadside thickets and at forest edges in the Northwest; breeding birds can be found at Stokes State Forest, Worthington State Forest, and on back roads along the Delaware River. The bright, cheerful song can be very similar to that of many Yellow Warblers, but typically stresses the second-to-last note: *seet-seet-seeSEEya.*

Clear dull white beneath, greenish above with bright white crown, white eye ring. Wingbars tinged yellow.

Medium-long tail often cocked, wing drooped. Spring male with reddish sides, black moustache.

Magnolia Warbler

Setophaga magnolia

L 5″ | **WS** 7.5″ | **WT** 0.3 OZ (8.7 G)

Soft blue and yellow, with a dramatic and distinctive tail pattern, the beautiful Magnolia Warbler is a common May and August migrant statewide, with a few breeding in some years in spruces in northwestern New Jersey. It can be found at Garret Mountain, Princeton, Palmyra, and any migration hotspot, often feeding low and in the open. The call is a quiet, nasal *chev*. The soft song, often heard on spring migration, is a whistled *wee-wee-weeo*, like a distant Hooded Warbler's.

Small and stocky. Gray head with white eye ring, neat white wingbars. Lemon underparts with long black streaks.

Base of tail white, tip broadly black. Spring male with black mask, bold white eye stripe, long black stripes on underparts.

Cape May Warbler

Setophaga tigrina

L 5″ | **WS** 8.25″ | **WT** 0.39 OZ (11 G)

The small, very fine-billed Cape May Warbler is a scarce spring migrant and an uncommon fall migrant throughout the state. Look for it in May and September, especially in pines and other conifers, at Garret Mountain, Princeton, and other migration hotspots—but do not expect to see this species at Cape May, its name notwithstanding. The song is an even series of very high-pitched whistles *seep-seep-seep-seep*; the call is a sparrow-like *tseet*.

Small and short-tailed, with fine, slightly downcurved bill. Dull yellow rump. Yellow of throat curls behind face to create pale neck crescent.

Finely streaked black beneath. Spring male with large white wing patch, rusty cheek, black cap.

Black-throated Blue Warbler

Setophaga caerulescens

L 5.25" | **WS** 7.75" | **WT** 0.36 OZ (10.2 G)

Small, dark, and handsome, the underbrush-loving Black-throated Blue Warbler is a common May and September migrant throughout New Jersey and an uncommon breeder in the forests of the northwest; migrants occur in any wooded habitat, while nesting birds can be reliably found on laurel-clad hillsides at High Point, Stokes State Forest, and Worthington State Forest. The call is a flat, junco-like *dap*; the lazy song is a low-pitched, burry *zee-zee-zee-ZEEE*, similar to the songs of some White-crowned Sparrows.

Dark and stocky, with fairly short tail. Female with dull green underparts, dark cheek; often small white wing square just behind shoulder.

Extensively white tail feathers. Male blue above, with black face and flanks. Large white wing square just behind shoulder.

Yellow-rumped Warbler

Setophaga coronata

L 5.5″ │ **WS** 9.25″ │ **WT** 0.43 OZ (12.3 G)

The large, sturdy, and confiding Yellow-rumped Warbler is by
far the most common member of the family in New Jersey. An
abundant migrant in all habitats in April and May and again
from late September to November, this species also winters in
large numbers in coastal thickets, where it feasts on the fruits
of myrtle and poison ivy. In the warmer seasons, it is often seen
catching insects in flight, sometimes at great height. Recent
years have seen a few breeding pairs along the Delaware River
in extreme northwestern New Jersey. The familiar call note, one
of the characteristic sounds of spring and fall woodlands, is a
dry, wooden *chick*. The common song is a vague, slow trill, like a
ball bearing rolling around in a tin can.

Young and winter birds
brown and streaked.
Yellow patch at side of
breast; rump often
concealed by folded
wing. White tail corners
visible in flight.

Sturdy legs, thick bill. White of throat curls onto side of neck. White line from bill to behind eye.

Spring male blue-gray with black streaks above and below. White throat and eye stripe set off broad black mask.

Black-throated Green Warbler

Setophaga virens

L 5″ | **WS** 7.75″ | **WT** 0.31 OZ (8.8 G)

A common migrant throughout the state in May and from late August to October, the colorful Black-throated Green Warbler breeds uncommonly in the northwest and the Pine Barrens; look for nesting pairs in conifers at High Point, Stokes State Forest, and Byrne State Forest. This species tends to feed high in trees, but migrants may descend to eye level. The call is a distinctive dry *tikt*, the song a pleasant buzzing whistle *zee-zee-ZOO-zoo-zee*.

Fairly bulky and long-tailed. Dull green above, with bright yellow face and black-streaked white underparts.

White outer tail feathers. Adult male with black throat and breast.

Cerulean Warbler

Setophaga cerulea

L 4.75″ | **WS** 7.75″ | **WT** 0.33 OZ (9.3 G)

Rapidly declining over much of its range, the treetop-loving
Cerulean Warbler is still locally common in northwestern
New Jersey, where it breeds in old forests of tall oaks, tulips,
and sycamores. Males arrive in late April and sing into June,
after which the silent birds are very difficult to find; they
leave the state in August for their narrow wintering grounds in
northern South America. Singing males are readily heard
and, with patience, seen, in High Point State Park and Stokes
State Forest and along the upper Delaware River; migrants
are occasionally detected at Cape May, Princeton, or Garret
Mountain, especially in May. The distinctive three-parted song
begins with a low, rolling trill, followed by two long ascending
buzzes: *trtrtr bzz beeez.*

Small but stout, with fairly
short tail and large head.
White underparts, well-defined
white wingbars and bluish
crown; female greenish above.

Adult male sky
blue above with
neatly striped
flanks and fine
black breast band.

Blackburnian Warbler

Setophaga fusca

L 5″ | **WS** 8.5″ | **WT** 0.34 OZ (9.8 G)

The small, often furtive Blackburnian Warbler is a fairly
common spring and fall migrant throughout New Jersey; its
abundance is masked by its habit of feeding high in treetop
foliage, where it can be very hard to see. A few pairs are found
breeding along the Delaware River and in the mountains
of northwestern New Jersey, especially at High Point and in
Worthington State Forest. The song is a series of very high,
thin notes that introduce a high-pitched trill *tse-tse-TSIPP*,
recalling a falsetto Northern Parula.

Compact and
colorful, with
white-striped back
and complex face
pattern: colorful
crown, eye stripe,
and side of neck.

Spring male with
bright orange and
black head pattern.

Yellow-throated Warbler

Setophaga dominica

L 5.5″ | **WS** 8″ | **WT** 0.33 OZ (9.4 G)

Large, long-billed, and deliberate, the Yellow-throated Warbler
is a locally common breeding bird in southern pines; look for it
from late March to August creeping slowly up trunks and along
branches at Jakes Landing and Belleplain State Forest. A few
also breed in deciduous woods along the Delaware River north
of Trenton. The loud, sweet chip resembles that of an outsized
Yellow Warbler; the lovely song is a liquid descending whistle
dwee-dwee-dwoo-dwoo-dwo.

Bulky and heavy-billed,
with solid gray back
and neat yellow throat
and upper breast.
Usually seen on large
branches or trunks.

Solid gray crown, large
white eye stripe and
neck patch. Yellow
throat set off by broad
black moustache.

Prairie Warbler

Setophaga discolor

L 4.75″ | **WS** 7″ | **WT** 0.27 OZ (7.7 G)

A characteristic species of old fields, especially those with
tangled red cedar, the bright yellow, tail-wagging Prairie
Warbler is a common breeding bird over most of New Jersey.
Migrants can be seen in May and September nearly anywhere,
and nesting birds are reliably seen at Stokes State Forest,
Belleplain, and Cape May. Usually seen low in the dense
vegetation they prefer, Prairie Warblers give a dull *tuk* call and
a very distinctive, loud song, a long series of discrete buzzing
notes running up the scale.

Small. Complex face pattern
with conspicuous pale eye
crescents, dark curve below
eye. Bobs long tail incessantly.

Greenish above,
entire underparts
lemon yellow with
black streaks on
side of breast and
flanks. Adult male
with yellow and
black face pattern.

Palm Warbler

Setophaga palmarum

L 5.5″ | **WS** 8″ | **WT** 0.36 OZ (10.3 G)

Among the first spring warblers to arrive and the last fall warblers to leave, the sturdy Palm Warbler is a common migrant in April and again in October. A few winter most years, especially along the coast; migrants are easily found at Sandy Hook, Garret Mountain, Glenhurst, and Cape May. This species is most often seen near or on the ground, where it wags its tail unceasingly. The call is a slightly liquid, low chip; the song, occasionally given by spring migrants, is a buzzy, low-pitched trill.

Fairly large, with long legs and tail. Feeds on ground, wagging tail. Rump and undertail yellowish, broad white stripe over eye.

Underparts vary from gray to yellow; coarsely streaked. Adult with bright rusty cap.

Pine Warbler

Setophaga pinus

L 5.5″ | **WS** 8.75″ | **WT** 0.42 OZ (12 G)

Large and, by warbler standards, lethargic, the modestly colored Pine Warbler is a common, notably early spring migrant throughout New Jersey, frequenting both conifers and deciduous trees in March and April; breeding birds, which do prefer pines, are more common in the south. Pine Warblers linger into November, and some winter each year in southern areas, often visiting feeders for suet. The call is a metallic *dit*, the song a long, vague trill, recalling that of a junco or an unskilled Chipping Sparrow.

Large and sturdy, with heavy bill. Unstreaked back, neat white wingbars, yellowish breast and throat. Dark cheek, broken eye ring.

Feeds methodically on large branches and cones. White outer tail feathers, white belly, vague breast streaking. Adult male with bright yellow throat and breast.

Bay-breasted Warbler

Setophaga castanea

L 5.5″ | **WS** 9″ | **WT** 0.44 OZ (12.5 G)

Chunky and short-tailed, the dark Bay-breasted Warbler is an uncommon May and September migrant throughout New Jersey; it can be seen at Garret Mountain, Palmyra, and Cape May, where it stays high in the trees in spring, coming lower in fall. Like Tennessee and Cape May Warblers, numbers of this species vary significantly as spruce budworm populations rise and fall on the breeding grounds. The song is a very high-pitched chant *seea-seea-seea*, thinner than that of the Black-and-white Warbler; the common call is a sharp *dzt*.

Streaked back, broad white wingbars, dingy beneath including undertail. Dark legs and toes. Sides often warm buff in fall.

Large and sturdy, with short bill. Pale side of neck contrasts with darker cheek. Adult male with chestnut crown, throat, and sides.

Blackpoll Warbler

Setophaga striata

L 5.5″ | **WS** 9″ | **WT** 0.46 OZ (13 G)

Large and short-tailed, the streaky Blackpoll Warbler is a
common migrant throughout the state, arriving in mid-May and
again in mid-September; fall birds usually appear later than
most Bay-breasted Warblers and linger later into the season,
sometimes into November. Especially in autumn, this species is
generally more common at coastal sites than inland. In spring,
look for it high in the trees at Garret Mountain, Princeton,
Great Swamp NWR, and Cape May; in fall, when Blackpolls
feed at all heights, Sandy Hook, Island Beach, and Cape May
are reliable localities. The song is an urgent, high-pitched,
scratchy phrase, accelerating in the middle: *tssi-tssi-tssitssi-
tssi.* The commonly heard call is a buzzing *tzip.*

Streaked back and underparts,
broad white wingbars,
dull white or yellowish beneath
with clear white undertail.
Yellow toes.

Stocky and stumpy-tailed, with short, thick bill. Thin black line through eye creates stern facial expression.

Spring male boldly streaked black above and below. Broad white wingbars, white cheek, solid black cap.

Snow Bunting
Plectrophenax nivalis

L 6.75″ | **WS** 14″ | **WT** 1.5 OZ (42 G)

Restless and shy, the chunky, short-tailed Snow Bunting is a fairly common winter bird on New Jersey's beaches and open farmlands, where sometimes large flocks flit nervously low over the ground. From November to February, this species can be found at Sandy Hook, Island Beach, and Barnegat Light, often in the company of Horned Larks; Alpha and the large northern reservoirs are good inland sites. The typical call is a short whistle *phew*.

Large and round, with tiny bill. Very long wings with white patches conspicuous in flight. Crouching posture when feeding.

White head marked rusty in winter. Larger, shorter-tailed, and much whiter than Horned Larks, with which it often flocks.

Lapland Longspur

Calcarius lapponicus

L 6.25″ | **WS** 11.5″ | **WT** 0.95 OZ (27 G)

A stout, long-winged winter bird of open country, the richly colored Lapland Longspur can be found in very small numbers, usually with Horned Larks or Snow Buntings, on farm fields and, especially, dunes and beaches from November to March. Cape May, Barnegat Light, and Sandy Hook are reliable sites, but even there it is unusual to see more than one or two individuals creeping on bent legs through the grass. In flight, when the dark tail distinguishes them from Snow Buntings, Lapland Longspurs give a down-slurred whistle and a short, dry rattle.

Superficially sparrow-like, but long-winged and thick-billed. Short, blackish tail with white edges; black triangle outlines cheek.

Well-marked winter birds show rusty hind neck and black smudge on breast. Long hind claw.

Eastern Towhee

Pipilo erythrophthalmus

L 8.5″ | **WS** 10.5″ | **WT** 1.4 OZ (40 G)

The largest sparrow in the eastern US and Canada, the dark, long-tailed Eastern Towhee is a common breeding bird in overgrown fields and dense woodland edge across New Jersey; it is especially abundant in the Pine Barrens. Look for this colorful species scratching noisily on the forest floor from mid-April to October at High Point, Great Swamp NWR, Byrne State Forest, and Brigantine NWR. Migrants occur in any wooded habitat, including urban parks and suburban feeders; fall birds linger into November, and wintering individuals are common in the southern half of the state. The loud calls include a sizzling *tzzr* and a metallic, rising *t'WHEE*; the ringing, clearly phrased song, given from a conspicuous perch, ends in a long, quavering trill *chweek-twa-TEEE*.

Large, portly sparrow. Adult's rusty sides contrast with clean white belly. Adult female chocolate brown above.

Large white tail spots in all plumages. Long, wide tail and thick, conical bill. Deep red eye. Adult male rich black above.

Field Sparrow
Spizella pusilla

L 5.75″ | **WS** 8″ | **WT** 0.44 OZ (12.5 G)

The tiny, long-tailed Field Sparrow is a common breeding bird in overgrown fields throughout the state; migrants are conspicuous in April and October, but good numbers are present all year in much of the state. Look for nesting birds at Great Swamp NWR, Negri-Nepote, and Cape May. The common call note is a surprisingly robust, metallic *tsek*. The silvery song is one of New Jersey's most beautiful bird vocalizations, an accelerating series of sweet chips; some birds sing a slower, ascending song similar to that of the Prairie Warbler.

Very small, long-tailed and small-billed. Rusty back, crown, and stripe behind eye; pinkish bill and legs.

Thin white wingbars; notched tail blackish above. Fine white eye ring creates open, "innocent" facial expression.

American Tree Sparrow

Spizella arborea

L 6.25" | **WS** 9.5" | **WT** 0.7 OZ (20 G)

Medium-sized and long-tailed, the rusty American Tree Sparrow is a fairly common wintering species in brushy habitats in the northern two thirds of New Jersey; most birds arrive in November and are gone by the end of March. Often found with juncos and other sparrows, this species can be found at DeKorte Park, Great Swamp NWR, and Glenhurst. Among its calls are a long, even *speet* and a rollicking *teetle*; the lively song *tee-tee-tee-tettle-ee* is occasionally heard on warm winter days.

Long tail with poorly defined white edge. Thick-based, rather long bill with yellow base. Gray head with rusty cap and eye line.

Chipping Sparrow
Spizella passerina

L 5.5″ | **WS** 8.5″ | **WT** 0.42 OZ (12 G)

The small, delicate Chipping Sparrow is a common and familiar
breeder throughout New Jersey, nesting in dense evergreens
in suburban yards, urban parks, and pine forests. Arrival is
in early April, with most birds departing in October, though
increasing numbers spend the winter in the state, especially
in the south. Outside of the breeding season, this gregarious
species can be found in flocks feeding quietly on lawns and
woodland edges, often mixing with other sparrows; migrants
and winterers visit bird feeders. If startled, these flocks fly
swiftly into the outer branches of small trees, giving high-
pitched, slightly upslurred *tsee* notes. The song is a simple
chipping trill, steadier than that of juncos and usually slower
and lower-pitched than that of the Pine Warbler.

Very small and
slender, with long tail,
small head, and
pointed bill. Even gray
underparts, fine
eye ring, dark eye line.

Deep tail notch, silvery rump. Fine eye ring split by dark line from bill to back of head. Juvenile with fine streaking below.

Breeding adult with bright rusty cap, dark bill, broad white stripe over eye.

Swamp Sparrow
Melospiza georgiana

L 5.75″ | **WS** 7.25″ | **WT** 0.6 OZ (17 G)

Dark and robust, with a long, rounded tail, the handsome Swamp Sparrow is a common migrant and wintering bird in brushy habitats across the state; breeding birds are found wherever fresh or saltwater marshes support abundant cattails or reeds, including Vernon Crossing, DeKorte Park, Great Swamp NWR, Brigantine NWR, and Cape May. The distinctive calls include a buzzy *tzert* and a rich, bright, phoebe-like *stlip*; the song, often heard in marshes at night, is a leisurely trill, fuller and lower-pitched than that of the Chipping Sparrow.

Dark rusty above, with gray face; grayish, variably streaked underparts often with breast spot, white throat.

Portly, with long tail, large head, fairly large bill. Young and winter adult with gray central crown stripe.

Lincoln's Sparrow

Melospiza lincolnii

L 5.75″ | **WS** 7.5″ | **WT** 0.6 OZ (17 G)

The shy but colorful Lincoln's Sparrow is an uncommon migrant across the state, much more frequently seen in fall than on the northbound migration in May. Fond of thick brush piles and dark thickets, this species can be seen in October at Garret Mountain, Glenhurst, Palmyra, and Cape May. The calls include a buzzy *tzeet* similar to that of the Swamp Sparrow and a flat, junco-like *tep*. The remarkable song, a slurred phrase followed by wren-like trills, is occasionally heard on migration.

Medium-sized. Long tail, thin bill; crest often raised. Fine streaks above and below, gray face with thin eye ring. Gray central crown stripe.

Yellowish wash across breast and flank; yellowish stripe borders throat. Fine, regular streaking continues down flank.

Song Sparrow
Melospiza melodia

L 6.25″ | **WS** 8.25″ | **WT** 0.7 OZ (20 G)

New Jersey's most abundant sparrow, the Song Sparrow is a rotund, chocolate-brown bird with a long, rounded tail that it wags in flight. A common breeder in all wooded or brushy habitats throughout the state, it is especially fond of marsh edges and lakeshores; this species often visits backyard feeders, and nests happily in suburbs and urban parks. Song Sparrows do not form large flocks, but during migration associate loosely with other species in overgrown fields. The calls include a brief, emphatic *tsip* and a low-pitched, husky *jub*. The loud, cheerful song is given from an exposed perch; it begins with clear whistles, followed by a long buzz that introduces a series of rolling phrases *tee-tee-tee-TRRR-tiddlea-tiddlea*.

Chocolate brown wings and tail contrast with broad gray eye stripe.

Medium-sized. Full-breasted, with long tail, large bill. White underparts with coarse, irregular streaks; often large breast spot.

Vesper Sparrow

Pooecetes gramineus

L 6.25″ | **WS** 10″ | **WT** 0.91 OZ (26 G)

Unobtrusive and uncommon, the streaky Vesper Sparrow can be found in very small numbers in October feeding quietly on the ground at Glenhurst, Coldbrook Reserve, Sandy Hook, and Cape May; an endangered breeder in the state, a few pairs still nest in grassy fields and pastures in northwestern New Jersey. The call is a thin, short *seep*. The song, rarely heard except on the breeding grounds, begins with loud, clear whistles and ends in a loose musical trill.

Heavy line beneath cheek gives jowly appearance. White belly surrounded by blurry brown streaks on flank and breast; often small breast spot.

Medium-large, with wide, square tail and swollen bill. Outer tail feathers white; white eye ring on brown face.

Fox Sparrow

Passerella iliaca

L 7″ | **WS** 10.5″ | **WT** 1.1 OZ (32 G)

The bright, heavily marked Fox Sparrow is the largest of our "brown" sparrows. A common migrant throughout New Jersey forests in late October and November, this species winters locally in the southern half of the state, departing in March. Migrants are seen at Garret Mountain, Great Swamp NWR, and Trenton Marsh; wintering birds are reliable at Cape May. The calls include a long, even *tseee* and a harsh, blackbird-like *chack*; spring birds sing a loud, melodic *twee-atweea-tzee*.

Very large, with fairly long tail and heavy, yellow-based bill. Wings and tail foxy red, head gray.

White underparts with rusty chevrons, usually coalescing into large central breast spot.

Savannah Sparrow

Passerculus sandwichensis

L 5.5″ | **WS** 6.75″ | **WT** 0.7 OZ (20 G)

The small, short-tailed, crisply marked Savannah Sparrow is a common migrant in April and October on open fields and beaches throughout the state; small numbers winter, especially in southern New Jersey. Now a very rare breeder, nesting Savannah Sparrows occur erratically at such sites as Walkill NWR, Negri-Nepote, and Duke Farms. Migrants are easily found at Liberty State Park, Glenhurst, Palmyra, Brigantine NWR, and Cape May. The large, pale birds that winter in the dunes at Island Beach, Barnegat Light, and Stone Harbor are Ipswich Sparrows, a distinctive geographic variant of the Savannah Sparrow sometimes considered a separate species. Savannah Sparrows call with a high, thin, short *tsp*; the song, only rarely heard away from the breeding grounds, is a simple *tsippup CHZZ chzz*.

Small and slender, with short, noticeably notched tail and slender bill. Back with white stripes. Eye stripe often tinged yellow.

White underparts with
fine blackish streaks.
Thin white central
crown stripe.

Ipswich Sparrow large
and frosty, with blurry
brown streaks below.

Grasshopper Sparrow

Ammodramus savannarum

L 5″ | **WS** 7.75″ | **WT** 0.6 OZ (17 G)

Small, with a short tail and thick, outsized bill, the long-legged Grasshopper Sparrow is a scarce and local breeder in grassy fields and pastures; Negri-Nepote, Walkill NWR, and Duke Farms are good places to look and listen for this somewhat secretive species. Migrants are rarely seen, but occur annually at Sandy Hook, Glenhurst, and Cape May. The quiet, high-pitched songs include an insect-like *tipip-ZEEE* and an out-of-control warble, alternately squeaking and sizzling.

Small and front-heavy, with very short tail and large head and bill. Back richly colored brown, black, white. Buffy head with yellowish eye stripe.

Long, thick legs. Strong blackish crown stripes, buffy face. Adult underparts unstreaked yellowish-buff.

Seaside Sparrow

Ammodramus maritimus

L 6″ | **WS** 7.5″ | **WT** 0.81 OZ (23 G)

The large, dark, spike-billed Seaside Sparrow is fairly common in New Jersey's coastal saltmarshes from April to November; a few may winter on the nesting grounds in some years. Fond of tall cordgrass, Seaside Sparrows are easy to see during the breeding season at Brigantine NWR, Nummy Island, and Jakes Landing, where they feed on the mud of tidal channels and sing from low but conspicuous perches. The song is a loud stuttering buzz *ktta-CHEE*.

Large and long-billed, with fairly short tail. Somber gray head with bright white throat and yellowish spot above eye.

Stays deep in marsh vegetation except when feeding on mud or singing from exposed perch.

Saltmarsh Sparrow

Ammodramus caudacutus

L 5.25″ | **WS** 7″ | **WT** 0.67 OZ (19 G)

Fairly large, long-billed, and colorful, Saltmarsh Sparrows are uncommon and often reclusive breeding birds in New Jersey's coastal saltmarshes from April to October; a few winter in the south in most years. With patience, they can be found feeding mouse-like in low cordgrass at Brigantine NWR, Tuckerton, and the Raritan Bay saltmarshes. The quiet, inconspicuous, and rarely heard song is a vague series of soft buzzes.

Short, spiky tail and long, thin, almost blackbird-like bill. Dark gray cheek surrounded by bright orange; heavily streaked white underparts.

Nelson's Sparrow

Ammodramus nelsoni

L 5″ | **WS** 7″ | **WT** 0.6 OZ (17 G)

Very similar to the Saltmarsh Sparrow, with which it often occurs, the colorful Nelson's Sparrow is a fairly common migrant in coastal marshes; unlike the Saltmarsh Sparrow, it also occurs in small numbers inland. Sandy Hook, Tuckerton, and Cold Brook are likely sites to find this species in October and November; it is much more rarely seen in spring migration, and seems to be scarce in winter, when Tuckerton is usually the best place to seek this bird.

Buffier breast, blurrier streaking than Saltmarsh. Migrants from inland populations extensively orange on breast.

Dark-eyed Junco

Junco hyemalis

L 6.25″ | **WS** 9.25″ | **WT** 0.67 OZ (19 G)

The pudgy, white-bellied, pink-billed Dark-eyed Junco may be New Jersey's most common winter sparrow, an abundant visitor from October to April at woodland edge and in weedy fields; sociable and confiding, juncos join White-throated and other sparrows hopping and scratching on the ground in urban parks and beneath suburban feeders across the state. Spring migrants often feed surprisingly high in newly leafed trees. A very few nest some years at High Point, Stokes State Forest, or other northwestern sites. The varied calls include a dull *dit*, a low-pitched *tup*, and an abrupt, sharp *tzit* when the birds fly off, their brilliant white outer tail feathers flashing. The song, often heard on warm spring days, is a slow, dull, descending trill *dddd-ddd-d*.

Fairly large and fat, with white belly, large gray head, and small pink bill. White outer tail often flashed when feeding.

Extensive white in tail from beneath. Adult male dark slaty above, blackest on head.

Wings usually without wing bars. Tail dark slate from above.

White-throated Sparrow

Zonotrichia albicollis

L 6.75" | **WS** 9" | **WT** 0.91 OZ (26 G)

One of New Jersey's most abundant winter birds, the bold, pot-bellied White-throated Sparrow is found in brushy and forested habitats throughout the state from October to April, often visiting feeders in company with juncos and other sparrows. The late fall flight at Cape May and other coastal hotspots can involve numbers well into the thousands. In some years a few stay to breed in northwestern forests; High Point and Stokes State Forest are the most frequent nesting sites. A noisy species even in winter, the White-throated Sparrow's calls include a long, hissing *ssseee* and a bright, almost cardinal-like *tchip*. The familiar song is often heard during spring migration or on warm winter days, a musical, well-cadenced series of sharply separated whistles *dee-DEE-deedeedee*.

Very large and long-tailed; "neckless" with large head, thick bill. Heavily striped head, white throat set off from gray breast. Yellow spot between eye and bill.

Dark bill in all plumages. Pale central crown stripe, very broad white or tan stripe above eye towards nape.

White-crowned Sparrow

Zonotrichia leucophrys

L 7″ | **WS** 9.5″ | **WT** 1 OZ (29 G)

Very large, with a long tail and neck and small, slightly crested head, the elegant White-crowned Sparrow is a fairly common fall and uncommon spring migrant on brushy field edges across New Jersey; small numbers winter in the south. Migrants can be found in October and, less reliably, in early May at Glenhurst, Cold Brook, Brigantine NWR, and Cape May. The calls include a bright chip and a descending *seep*; spring birds sing a buzzing *zee-zee-ZHH-zhh*.

As large as Fox Sparrow, with long tail, deep belly, and long, often outstretched neck. Bold head stripes, gray throat and breast.

Orange or reddish bill in all plumages. Adult with black and white head stripes.

Sparrows

Like shorebirds, sparrows are more easily identified by habitat, shape, and behavior than by their often cryptic brown plumages. For example, a small sparrow breeding in a field of tall grass and sparse shrubs is probably a Grasshopper Sparrow or a Field Sparrow; the former has a short tail and large head, the latter a long tail and small head. A chubby, long-tailed sparrow diving into shadowy brush is likely a White-throated Sparrow, while a similar bird flushing to the open top of a bush or short tree may be a White-crowned Sparrow. Song Sparrows often feed in the open; Lincoln's Sparrows are more likely to be in cover.

Most sparrows show a streaked breast in some plumage. This bird's broad tail, round belly, and large bill eliminate many possibilities; the rusty wing identifies it as a Swamp Sparrow.

The Chipping Sparrow shares many of the Swamp Sparrow's colors and patterns, but note the long, slender tail, flat belly, and tiny bill.

Scarlet Tanager

Piranga olivacea

L 7″ | **WS** 11.5″ | **WT** 0.98 OZ (28 G)

An inconspicuous, slow-moving species of shady treetops, the short-tailed, small-billed Scarlet Tanager is a common migrant throughout New Jersey and a fairly common breeder in conifers and deciduous forests. Migrants, which often form loose flocks with warblers, grosbeaks, and orioles, are easily found in May and September at Garret Mountain, Princeton, Palmyra, and wooded urban parks; nesting birds are widespread from High Point to the southern Pine Barrens, preferring tall trees in established woodlands, where they can be surprisingly difficult to see in the foliage. The typical call is a low, toneless *chap*, often followed by a rough buzz *chap-brrr*. The slow, hoarse song is robin-like in pattern but buzzy, a leisurely caroling phrase *brzha-brzhee-brzhap*.

Size of a large sparrow, with short, dark tail, large head, and short, dark bill.

Dark wings and tail contrast with uniform body and bland face.

Spring and summer adult male red with black wings and tail. Young male patched with green; wings browner.

Summer Tanager

Piranga rubra

L 7.75″ | **WS** 12″ | **WT** 1 OZ (29 G)

The large-billed, uniformly colored Summer Tanager is an uncommon breeder at scattered locations in the Pine Barrens and a scarce migrant, most frequently encountered in southern New Jersey in early May. Nesting birds can be found in mixed oaks and pines at Belleplain and Dividing Creek; spring migrants occur in very small numbers irregularly north to Sandy Hook and Garret Mountain. The distinctive call is a stuttering chuckle *piddaduck*; the robin-like song is more exuberant and less hoarse than that of the Scarlet Tanager.

Larger and longer-tailed than Scarlet. Wings and tail not strikingly darker than body and bland face.

Lanky and long-billed. Adult male rose red, younger birds patched green.

Rose-breasted Grosbeak

Pheucticus ludovicianus

L 8″ | **WS** 12.5″ | **WT** 1.6 OZ (45 G)

Fist-shaped, with a square head and massive triangular bill, the lethargic Rose-breasted Grosbeak is a common migrant throughout New Jersey and a fairly common breeding bird in open woodlands in the northern half of the state. Migrants can be found in May and September at Garret Mountain, Sandy Hook, and Cape May; nesting birds are reliable at High Point, Stokes State Forest, and Ringwood, among other sites. The distinctive call is an almost painfully squeaky *pleek*. The beautiful song is a long, sweet, warbling carol.

Short wing with white wing bar; huge, pale bill. Female, young, and winter birds with dramatically striped head, coarsely streaked breast.

Short, broad tail with white spots in adult male. Spring and summer male with black head, red triangle on breast.

Northern Cardinal
Cardinalis cardinalis

L 8.75″ | **WS** 12″ | **WT** 1.6 OZ (45 G)

Abundant, noisy, and strikingly plumaged, the black-faced,
long-tailed Northern Cardinal is a permanent resident of
brushy woods, urban parks, and suburban yards throughout
New Jersey. This species is fiercely territorial in the breeding
season, but forms loose flocks with other ground-foraging birds
on forest edges and at feeders the rest of the year. Generally
found close to the ground and near thick cover, cardinals mount
high exposed perches to sing in winter and spring, starting
as early as late December. The usual call is a loud, sharp,
penetrating *pink*, sometimes extended into a rapid, rattling
series by agitated birds. The very loud, rich song is a variable
series of slurred whistles; a typical song begins with ascending
notes, followed by a faster group of descending slurs.

Size of a large sparrow,
with long tail, silky body
plumage, crested head, huge
triangular bill. Female olive
brown with red highlights.

Juvenile with darker bill, very little black on face.

Adult male scarlet red, with greenish cast to wings and back.

Blue Grosbeak

Passerina caerulea

L | 6.75" | WS | 11" | **WT** 0.98 OZ (28 G)

Rapidly increasing and spreading north, the handsome Blue Grosbeak is a fairly common breeder in southern New Jersey and an uncommon migrant in May and from August to October throughout the state. Breeding birds are found at Six Mile Run, Negri-Nepote, and Cape May; migrants can occur anywhere in overgrown fields. The call of this sometimes secretive species is a bright, metallic *plink*. The quiet song, given from a wire or dead branch, is a long, low-pitched, grumbling warble.

Stout, with large head and large, pointed bill. Fairly short, broad tail often flicked. Bright chestnut wingbars.

Spring and summer adult male dull purplish-black with black face. Colorful wings, large bill unlike Indigo Bunting.

Indigo Bunting
Passerina cyanea

L 5.5″ | **WS** 8″ | **WT** 0.51 OZ (14.5 G)

Small and pointy-faced, the fairly long-tailed, slender-billed Indigo Bunting is a common breeder and migrant throughout New Jersey. Look for it from May to October in weedy fields and on roadside wires at High Point, Glenhurst, Negri-Nepote, and Cape May. Usually conspicuous and confiding, this species calls a buzzy *dzeet* and a flat, faintly metallic *tik*. Males sing on even the hottest summer days, a series of wiry paired notes at different pitches *wiwi-tweetwee-dudu*.

Slender, with small head and relatively slender, faintly curved bill. Fairly short, narrow tail often flicked. Poorly defined whitish or bluish wingbars.

Spring and summer adult male bright blue-black with darker head. Uniformly blue wings, small bill. Young males patchy blue and brown.

Bobolink

Dolichonyx oryzivorus

L 7″ | **WS** 11.5″ | **WT** 1.5 OZ (43 G) | ♂ > ♀

The spike-tailed, thick-billed Bobolink is a common migrant from August to October, most abundant coastally; it is less common in May, and small numbers breed in weedy fields in the northern part of the state. Migrants can be found at Brigantine NWR, Cape May, and Palmyra. Nesting sites shift from year to year, but can include Walkill NWR and Negri-Nepote. The flight call is a sharp *spink*, the remarkable song, often given in flight, a long series of bubbling phrases.

Size of large sparrow, with short, spiky tail and thick, pointed bill. Female and fall male yellowish beneath, with heavily marked head.

Broad stripes on upper back. Spring and summer male with white lower back, creamy nape, black underparts.

Eastern Meadowlark

Sturnella magna

L 9.5″ | **WS** 14″ | **WT** 3.2 OZ (90 G) | ♂ > ♀

Short-tailed, fat-bodied, and long-billed, the awkwardly shaped but colorful Eastern Meadowlark is an uncommon and local breeder in weedy fields; small numbers winter in the southern half of New Jersey, especially in saltmarshes. Breeders occur at Walkill NWR, Negri-Nepote, and other old farmland sites. Wintering birds are found at Island Beach, Brigantine NWR, and Jakes Landing. The calls include a thin, nasal *veek* and a fast, high-pitched rattle. The song, given from a wire or dead tree, is a whistled phrase *teeyaa-teeyee*.

Robin-sized, with very short, white-edged tail. Long, sturdy legs; long, sharp bill emerges from flat head. Cryptically patterned above, coarsely streaked flank.

Breeding birds bright yellow beneath with black breast patch.

Red-winged Blackbird

Agelaius phoeniceus

L 8.75″ | **WS** 13″ | **WT** 1.8 OZ (52 G) | ♂ > ♀

Abundant, noisy, and social, the sharp-billed Red-winged Blackbird is one of New Jersey's most common and most conspicuous birds. Found year-round, this species is also an abundant migrant in February and March and again in October, when enormous flocks range in undulating flight across marshes and fields, roosting in thick woodlands and suburban parks. Wintering birds are commoner coastally and in the south, but occur anywhere in the state where snow does not cover the feeding areas, which include feedlots, open fields, and wet woodland edges. The flight call is a rubbery *pluk*; perched birds also give a thin, buzzy *keer*. The familiar song is a sure sign of spring, a very loud, throaty *kakaKREE* sung from a tree or cattail stalk.

Larger than sparrows, with fairly long tail, dark plumage, square head, sharp-pointed bill.

Female and young heavily streaked below; pale, sometimes pinkish throat. Bold pale eye stripe.

Dark eye; thick, sharp bill. Male with yellow wing bar and large, often concealed red shoulder patch.

Rusty Blackbird

Euphagus carolinus

L 9″ | **WS** 14″ | **WT** 2.1 OZ (60 G) | ♂ > ♀

Uncommon and rapidly declining in numbers, the subtly handsome Rusty Blackbird is an inconspicuous fall migrant and winter resident across New Jersey, present from October to March on dark wooded ponds and field edges; spring birds, which pass through in March and April, are noisier and more gregarious. Look for this bright-eyed bird at Great Swamp NWR, Troy Meadows, and Cape May. The flight call is a slightly liquid *tuk*; the song, often given by entire flocks in springtime, is a squeaky, ascending *oogLEEK*.

Size of Red-winged, slightly slenderer and longer-tailed. Fall and winter birds rusty brown; broad eye stripe.

Yellow eye and fine, straight bill. Adult male flat gray-black with little gloss.

Boat-tailed Grackle

Quiscalus major

♂ **L** 16.5" | **WS** 23" | **WT** 8 OZ (215 G)
♀ **L** 14.5" | **WS** 17.5" | **WT** 4.2 OZ (120 G)

The large, very long-tailed Boat-tailed Grackle is a fairly common but local resident in coastal salt marshes from Delaware Bay and Cape May north to the mouth of the Raritan River. Breeding birds can be seen feeding in low cordgrass or on roadsides at Sandy Hook, Nummy Island, and Stone Harbor; winter flocks may gather on North Shore beaches and parking lots. The loud vocalizations include a variety of rattles, squeals, and buzzing notes.

Very large, with pale eye, heavy, curved bill and long tail. Female and young buffy brown beneath with blackish wing and tail.

Adult male blue-black with club-shaped tail.

Common Grackle

Quiscalus quiscula

L 12.5″ | **WS** 17″ | **WT** 4 OZ (115 G) | ♂ > ♀

One of New Jersey's most abundant and familiar birds, the large, long-tailed, and gregarious Common Grackle is a common resident of fields, swamps, woodland edges, and urban parks throughout the state. This species winters in large flocks in southern areas, with at least a few lingering most years in northern New Jersey as well. The northward migration begins as early as February; autumn flocks, seen from August to October, can contain many thousands of birds, often mixed with cowbirds and Red-winged Blackbirds. In flight, grackles keep to a steady course, with little of the rising and falling typical of the smaller blackbirds. The flight call is a low-pitched, dull *chak*. The song, given from the ground or from a conspicuous perch, is a slow crashing sound, rising in pitch: *krrSHAK*.

Large, with long neck and bill. Long, straight wings and very long tail with wedge-shaped tip.

Many adults bronzy on back and wings, with contrasting green and blue iridescence on head and neck.

Adult colorful, with bright yellow eye, blue and purple iridescence, tail with wedge-shaped tip.

Brown-headed Cowbird

Molothrus ater

L 7.5″ | **WS** 12″ | **WT** 1.5 OZ (44 G) | ♂ > ♀

Our smallest blackbird, the demurely plumaged Brown-headed Cowbird is a common breeding bird and locally common winterer across the state. Plump, round-headed, and short-billed, cowbirds are found in all but the most densely wooded habitats. They feed in small flocks on the ground, walking methodically across open fields and lawns, often with their moderately short tails raised above the back; they also visit feeders for sunflower seeds. The young are often seen begging from adult "foster parents" of other species, including warblers, sparrows, and thrushes; this fascinating breeding strategy is unique among New Jersey birds. Females give a low, throaty rattle in flight. The male's squeaky flight whistle is expanded into a gurgling song *gloo-GLOOK*, given while bowing forward with wings half-spread.

Fairly short tail, small head, triangular bill. Uniform plumage, faintly streaked in adult female. Long, dark legs.

Juvenile neatly scalloped above, finely streaked below. Whitish throat contrasts with tan-brown head.

Adult male glossy black with rich chocolate head.

Baltimore Oriole

Icterus galbula

L 8.75″ | **WS** 11.5″ | **WT** 1.2 OZ (33 G)

Slender and lanky, with a small head and sharply pointed bill, the colorful Baltimore Oriole is a common migrant and breeder across the entire state, arriving in late April and departing from most areas in early October. Migrants are readily found in May and in August and September at Garret Mountain, Palmyra, and Cape May; breeding birds are most common in the north, but can be seen in open woodlands and suburbs with tall trees anywhere in New Jersey. Brightly plumaged and noisy, this species is often first detected by its calls, which include a harsh rattle and a flute-like *too-wee*; the song is an abrupt series of loud, heavily accented, piping phrases most often given from a perch high in the forest canopy.

Fairly short tail, but lanky body with long head and bill. Yellowish to orange, with white bars on dark wing. Female with dark eye line.

Young male and some females with black on throat or side of head.

Spring and summer adult male orange and black, with orange tail edges.

Orchard Oriole

Icterus spurius

L 7.25″ | **WS** 9.5″ | **WT** 0.67 OZ (19 G)

Small, with a short, strongly curved bill, the warbler-like
Orchard Oriole is a fairly common breeder on wooded field
edges throughout New Jersey. More common in the south,
this species arrives in late April and leaves very early; most
have quietly departed by August. Look for migrants at Garret
Mountain, Princeton, and Cape May. Breeding birds can be
found at Negri-Nepote, Belleplain, and Dividing Creek. The
call is a blackbird-like *chuck*; the song is a complex phrase of
whistles and jangling notes.

Small and long-tailed.
Female lime yellow,
with white wing bars;
similar young male
with black throat.

Adult male black with
dull chestnut belly,
rump, and wing bar. Tail
entirely black.

Pine Siskin

Spinus pinus

L 5″ | **WS** 9″ | **WT** 0.53 OZ (15 G)

Goldfinch-like but streaky and sharp-billed, the tiny Pine Siskin is an irregularly common migrant and winter resident throughout New Jersey; abundant some years, it can be nearly absent in others. Look for flocks of this active, noisy finch in alders or sunflowers at High Point, Sandy Hook, and Cape May, or at urban feeders with goldfinches. A few breed in the Northwest in some years. The calls include scratchy chattering and a very buzzy, ascending *zhree*; the song is like a raspy goldfinch's.

Long wings, forked tail, sharp bill. Heavily streaked above and below, with neat white or yellow wingbars.

Variable amount of bright yellow in wing and at base of short tail, especially obvious in flight.

American Goldfinch

Spinus tristis

L 5″ | **WS** 9″ | **WT** 0.46 OZ (13 G)

The tiny, small-billed American Goldfinch is a common and gregarious breeding bird and migrant throughout New Jersey; winter numbers vary from year to year, but this species can usually be found anywhere in the state in brushy fields or at suburban feeders. Winter flocks often associate with chickadees and Pine Siskins. Breeding birds prefer open habitats with abundant flowers, especially thistles, which provide both food and a soft lining for the nest. Common calls include a rising, whining *vree*; flying birds are easily recognized by their extravagantly undulating flight and musical, popping calls *pe-did-o-dee*. The song, delivered from a low perch or wire, is a long, complex series of high-pitched trills and nasal slurs.

Smaller than sparrows, with short tail, small head, and small, conical bill. Dark wings and tail with extensive white markings.

Young, female, and winter birds greenish tan with yellow face.

White rump and undertail. Spring and summer male bright pale yellow with black cap, pinkish bill.

House Finch
Haemorhous mexicanus

L 6″ | **WS** 9.5″ | **WT** 0.74 OZ (21 G)

Sparrow-sized and drab, with a long tail, short wings, and stubby bill, the introduced House Finch is now an abundant resident across New Jersey in all but extensively wooded habitats. This noisy species is hard to miss in fields, parks, and even city streets, where it flocks with goldfinches and House Sparrows. The common call is a whining *tzheerp*. The very loud, musical song, delivered from treetops and rooftops, is a long scratchy phrase ending in an emphatic downward buzz.

Long tail square or slightly notched; small head, short wing, curved bill. Female with blurry streaks, blank face.

Relatively slender. Male with red breast and eye stripe, clearly streaked dull white flank.

Purple Finch

Haemorhous purpureus

L 6″ | **WS** 10″ | **WT** 0.88 OZ (25 G)

Sparrow-sized and neatly marked, with a short tail, long wings, and triangular bill, the Purple Finch is an irregularly common migrant and winter resident across New Jersey. Quiet and retiring, small groups feed in ash trees and berry-laden bushes from mid-October to April; a few remain to breed at High Point and at Stokes State Forest. The distinctive flight call is a dry, wooden *ptik*; perched birds give a musical down-slurred *cheery*. The quiet musical song, often delivered from within dense foliage, is a sweet, rambling warble with a mumbled ending.

Chunky. Adult male with rosy back, breast, head, and wing bars; sparsely streaked clear white flank.

Short, clearly notched tail; large square head, long wing, straight-edged bill. Female and young male with neat streaks, white-striped face.

House Sparrow
Passer domesticus

L 6.25″ | **WS** 9.5″ | **WT** 0.98 OZ (28 G)

Larger, bulkier, more coarsely patterned, and broader-tailed than most native sparrows, the introduced House Sparrow is an abundant resident across New Jersey. Tightly structured, noisy flocks are easily found in brushy fields and parks and at feeders in all but the most densely wooded habitats. Probably the most urban of our birds, House Sparrows are ubiquitous on city sidewalks, nesting in streetlights and cracks in buildings; in more pastoral settings, they may drive swallows or bluebirds from their cavities, or build bulky twig nests in low trees. If startled while feeding, House Sparrows fly clumsily into low dense bushes, landing in irregularly spaced clumps. The call is a loud, resonant *chirmp*, in early spring given in a long series as a song.

Short tail; large head, heavy swollen bill. Back with wide tawny stripes, wing with single white bar. Female dingy gray below, with broad buffy band from eye to nape.

Adult male with blue-gray crown, chestnut nape, black bill. Throat and upper breast solid black in spring and summer.

Male throat and breast clouded with dingy gray in fall and winter.

Author Acknowledgments

I've been fortunate over the past nearly 30 years to bird New Jersey with dozens of friends and colleagues, every one of whom has contributed to this book—most of them without even knowing it. I owe particularly much to Ted Floyd and to the late Dave Evans for wide-ranging and invariably thoughtful conversations whose traces are obvious, to me at least, on nearly every page here.

My thanks go, too, to the photographers without whose fine images this book would be both less attractive and less informative. My publishers, George Scott and Charles Nix, have been as skilled as they are gracious, making a complicated project proceed smoothly towards what I hope has been a satisfying conclusion for them, too.

This book, like all else, is dedicated to my favorite field companions, Alison Beringer, and Gellert.

—Rick Wright
Bloomfield, New Jersey
December 2013

Scott & Nix Acknowledgments

We thank Rick Wright for his excellent text, editorial acumen, expert birding experience, patience, and good spirit under deadlines. We thank Jeffrey Gordon and the entire board at the American Birding Association for all the good work they do for birders and birds. Special thanks to Curt Matthews at Independent Book Publishers (IPG) along with his colleagues, Joe Matthews, Mark Voigt, Jeff Palicki, Michael Riley, Mary Rowles, John Bouldry, and many others. We give enormous thanks to Brian E. Small for his extraordinary nature photography, and to the other photographers whose images illuminate this guide, including Mike Danzenbaker, Jim Zipp, Garth McElroy, Bob Steele, Alan Murphy, and Visual Resources for Ornithology (VIREO)/Academy of Natural Sciences.

Image Credits

(T) = Top, (B)=Bottom, (L)=Left, (R)=Right, (TL)=Top left, (TR)=Top right, (BL)=Bottom left, (BR)=Bottom right; pages with multiple images from one source are indicated by a single credit.

P. XIII Brian E. Small. **P. XVI** Brian E. Small. **P. XVIII** Brian E. Small. **P. XIX** Brian E. Small. **P. XXI** Brian E. Small. **P. XXI** Brian E. Small. **P. XXII** Mike Danzenbaker. **P. XXIII** Brian E. Small. **P. XXIV** Brian E. Small(T), Brian E. Small(BL), P. Moylan/VIREO(BR). **P. XXV** Brian E. Small. **P. XXVI** Brian E. Small. **P. XXVII** Brian E. Small. **P. XXVIII** Brian E. Small. **P. 2** Brian E. Small. **P. 3** Brian E. Small. **P. 4** Mike Danzenbaker. **P. 5** B. Schmoker/ VIREO. **P. 6** Brian E. Small. **P. 7** Brian E. Small. **P. 8** Alan Murphy. **P. 9** Brian E. Small. **P. 10** Brian E. Small. **P. 11** Brian E. Small(T), Mike Danzenbaker(B). **P. 12** Brian E. Small. **P. 13** Brian E. Small(T), Mike Danzenbaker(B). **P. 14** Jim Zipp. **P. 15** Jim Zipp(T), J. Jantunen/VIREO(B). **P. 16** Brian E. Small(T), Laure Neish/VIREO(B). **P. 17** Brian E. Small(T), A. Morris/VIREO(B). **P. 18** Brian E. Small. **P. 19** Brian E. Small(T), Mike Danzenbaker(B). **P. 20** Brian E. Small. **P. 21** Brian E. Small. **P. 22** Brian E. Small. **P. 23** Brian E. Small(T), Mike Danzenbaker(B). **P. 24** Mike Danzenbaker. **P. 25** Brian E. Small. **P. 26** Brian E. Small. **P. 27** Brian E. Small(T), Mike Danzenbaker(B). **P. 28** Brian E. Small. **P. 29** Brian E. Small. **P. 30** Brian E. Small. **P. 31** Brian E. Small. **P. 32** Brian E. Small. **P. 33** Mike Danzenbaker. **P. 34** Brian E. Small. **P. 35** Mike Danzenbaker. **P. 36** Brian E. Small. **P. 37** Brian E. Small. **P. 38** Mike Danzenbaker. **P. 39** Brian E. Small. **P. 40** Brian E. Small. **P. 41** Brian E. Small. **P. 42** Brian E. Small. **P. 43** Brian E. Small. **P. 44** Brian E. Small. **P. 45** Brian E. Small. **P. 46** Brian E. Small. **P. 47** Mike Danzenbaker. **P. 48** Mike Danzenbaker(T), Brian E. Small(B). **P. 49** Mike Danzenbaker(T), Brian E. Small(B). **P. 50** Brian E. Small. **P. 51** Brian E. Small(T), Mike Danzenbaker(B). **P. 52** Jim Zipp(T), G. Armistead/VIREO(B). **P. 53** Brian E. Small. **P. 54** Bob Steele(T), Brian E. Small(B). **P. 55** Mike Danzenbaker(T), Garth McElroy(B). **P. 56** Brian E. Small. **P. 57** Brian E. Small. **P. 58** Brian E. Small. **P. 59** Brian E. Small. **P. 60** Brian E. Small. **P. 61** Brian E. Small. **P. 62** Brian E. Small. **P. 63** Brian E. Small. **P. 64** Brian E. Small. **P. 65** Brian E. Small. **P. 66** Brian E. Small. **P. 67** Brian E. Small(T), Mike Danzenbaker(B). **P. 68** Brian E. Small. **P. 69** Brian E. Small(T), Mike Danzenbaker(B). **P. 70** Brian E. Small. **P. 71** Brian E. Small(T), Mike Danzenbaker(B). **P. 72** Brian E. Small(T), Mike Danzenbaker(B). **P. 73** Brian E. Small. **P. 74** Brian E. Small. **P. 75** Brian E. Small(TL), Mike Danzenbaker(TR), Brian E. Small(BR). **P. 76** Brian E. Small. **P. 77** Brian E. Small. **P. 78** Brian E. Small. **P. 79** Mike Danzenbaker. **P. 80** Brian E. Small. **P. 81** Brian E. Small. **P. 82** Brian E. Small. **P. 83** Jim Zipp. **P. 84** Jim Zipp. **P. 85** Jim Zipp. **P. 86** Jim Zipp. **P. 87** Jim Zipp. **P. 88** Mike Danzenbaker. **P. 89** J. Heidecker/VIREO. **P. 90** Jim Zipp. **P. 91** Brian E. Small. **P. 92** Brian E. Small(T), Mike Danzenbaker(B). **P. 93** Brian E. Small. **P. 94** Brian E. Small. **P. 95** Brian E. Small. **P. 96** Brian E. Small(T), Mike Danzenbaker(B). **P. 97** Brian E. Small(T), Mike Danzenbaker(B). **P. 98** Brian E. Small. **P. 99** Mike Danzenbaker(T), R. & S. Day/VIREO(B). **P. 100** Brian E. Small(T), Doug Wechsler/VIREO(B). **P. 101** Brian E. Small. **P. 102** Brian E. Small. **P. 103** Brian E. Small. **P. 104** Brian E. Small(T), Mike Danzenbaker(B). **P. 105** Brian E. Small(T), Mike Danzenbaker(B). **P. 106** Brian E. Small(T), Bob Steele(B). **P. 107** Brian E. Small. **P. 108** Brian E. Small. **P. 109** Brian E. Small(T), Mike Danzenbaker(B). **P. 110** Brian E. Small. **P. 111** Brian E. Small(T), Mike Danzenbaker(B). **P. 112** Brian E. Small. **P. 113** Brian E. Small. **P. 114** Brian E. Small(T), Mike Danzenbaker(B). **P. 115** Brian E. Small(T), Mike Danzenbaker(B). **P. 116** Brian E. Small. **P. 117** Brian E. Small. **P. 118** Brian E. Small. **P. 119** Brian E. Small. **P. 120** Brian E. Small. **P. 121** Jim Zipp(T), Mike Danzenbaker(B). **P. 122** Brian E. Small. **P. 123** E. Skrzypczak/VIREO(T), Brian E. Small(B). **P. 124** Mike Danzenbaker(T), Garth McElroy(B). **P. 125** Brian E. Small. **P. 126** Mike Danzenbaker. **P. 127** Brian E. Small. **P. 128** Brian E. Small. **P. 129** Brian E. Small(T), G. Bartley/VIREO(B). **P. 130** Mike Danzenbaker. **P. 131** Mike Danzenbaker(T), Brian E. Small(B). **P. 132** Mike Danzenbaker(T), Brian E. Small(B). **P. 133** Brian E. Small(T), Jim Zipp(B). **P. 134** Brian E. Small(T), Mike Danzenbaker(B). **P. 135** Mike Danzenbaker. **P. 136** Brian E. Small. **P. 137** Brian E. Small. **P. 138** Mike Danzenbaker(T), A. Morris/VIREO(B). **P. 139** Brian E. Small. **P. 140** Brian E. Small(T), Mike Danzenbaker(B). **P. 141** Brian E. Small(T), Mike Danzenbaker(B). **P. 142** Brian E. Small. **P. 143** Brian E. Small(T), Jim Zipp(B). **P. 144** Brian E. Small. **P. 145** Brian E. Small. **P. 146** Brian E. Small(L), D. Tipling/VIREO(R). **P. 147** Brian E. Small. **P. 148** Brian E. Small(L), R. & A. Simpson/ VIREO(R). **P. 149** Brian E. Small(L), A. Morris/VIREO(R). **P. 150** Brian E. Small. **P. 151** Brian E. Small. **P. 152** Alan Murphy. **P. 153** G. Bartley/VIREO. **P. 154** Brian E. Small(T), Mike Danzenbaker(B). **P. 155** Brian E. Small(L), G. Armistead/VIREO(R). **P. 156** Brian E. Small. **P. 157** Brian E. Small(L), G. Lasley/ VIREO(R). **P. 158** Brian E. Small(L), Alan Murphy(TR), R. Curtis/VIREO(BR). **P. 159** Brian E. Small. **P. 160** Brian E. Small. **P. 161** Mike Danzenbaker. **P. 162** Brian E. Small(L), J. Schumacher/VIREO(R). **P. 163** Brian E. Small(L), R. & N. Bowers/VIREO(R). **P. 164** Brian E. Small(L), K. Smith/VIREO(R). **P. 165** Jim Zipp(T), Mike Danzenbaker(B). **P. 166** Brian E. Small(L), Brian E. Small(T), Alan Murphy(BR). **P. 167** Jim Zipp(L),

Alan Murphy[TR] Alan Murphy[BR] **P. 168** Jim Zipp[T] Mike Danzenbaker[B] **P. 169** Brian E. Small.
P. 170 Brian E. Small. **P. 171** Brian E. Small. **P. 172** Brian E. Small. **P. 173** Brian E. Small. **P. 174** Brian E. Small.
P. 175 Brian E. Small[L] R. Curtis/VIREO[R] **P. 176** Brian E. Small. **P. 177** Brian E. Small. **P. 178** Brian E. Small.
P. 179 Brian E. Small. **P. 180** Brian E. Small. **P. 181** Brian E. Small. **P. 182** Brian E. Small[L] Jim Zipp[R]
P. 183 Brian E. Small. **P. 184** Brian E. Small. **P. 185** Alan Murphy. **P. 186** Jim Zipp. **P. 187** Brian E. Small.
P. 188 Brian E. Small[L] Mike Danzenbaker[R] **P. 189** Brian E. Small[L] Mike Danzenbaker[R]
P. 190 Mike Danzenbaker. **P. 191** G. Bartley/VIREO[L] A. Morris/VIREO[R] **P. 192** Mike Danzenbaker[T]
Brian E. Small[B] **P. 193** Brian E. Small[L] Mike Danzenbaker[R] **P. 194** Brian E. Small. **P. 195** Brian E. Small.
P. 196 Brian E. Small. **P. 197** Brian E. Small. **P. 198** Mike Danzenbaker. **P. 199** Brian E. Small.
P. 200 Brian E. Small. **P. 201** Brian E. Small. **P. 202** Brian E. Small. **P. 203** Brian E. Small. **P. 204** Brian E. Small.
P. 205 Brian E. Small. **P. 206** Brian E. Small. **P. 207** Brian E. Small. **P. 208** Brian E. Small. **P. 209** Brian E. Small.
P. 210 Brian E. Small. **P. 211** Brian E. Small. **P. 212** Brian E. Small. **P. 213** Brian E. Small. **P. 214** Brian E. Small.
P. 215 Brian E. Small. **P. 216** Brian E. Small. **P. 217** Brian E. Small. **P. 218** Brian E. Small. **P. 219** Brian E. Small.
P. 220 Brian E. Small. **P. 221** Brian E. Small[T] Mike Danzenbaker[B] **P. 222** Brian E. Small.
P. 223 Brian E. Small. **P. 224** Brian E. Small. **P. 225** R. & N. Bowers/VIREO. **P. 226** Brian E. Small.
P. 227 Brian E. Small. **P. 228** Brian E. Small. **P. 229** Brian E. Small. **P. 230** Brian E. Small. **P. 231** Brian E. Small.
P. 232 Brian E. Small. **P. 233** Brian E. Small. **P. 234** Brian E. Small. **P. 235** Brian E. Small. **P. 236** Brian E. Small.
P. 237 Brian E. Small. **P. 238** Brian E. Small. **P. 239** Brian E. Small. **P. 240** Brian E. Small. **P. 241** Brian E. Small.
P. 242 Brian E. Small. **P. 243** Brian E. Small. **P. 244** Brian E. Small. **P. 245** Brian E. Small. **P. 246** Brian E. Small.
P. 247 Brian E. Small. **P. 248** Brian E. Small. **P. 249** Brian E. Small[T] Mike Danzenbaker[B]
P. 250 Brian E. Small. **P. 251** Brian E. Small. **P. 252** Brian E. Small. **P. 253** Brian E. Small. **P. 254** Brian E. Small.
P. 255 Brian E. Small. **P. 256** Brian E. Small. **P. 257** Brian E. Small. **P. 258** Brian E. Small. **P. 259** Brian E. Small.
P. 260 Mike Danzenbaker[T] Brian E. Small[B] **P. 261** Brian E. Small. **P. 262** Brian E. Small.
P. 263 Brian E. Small. **P. 264** Brian E. Small. **P. 265** Brian E. Small. **P. 266** Mike Danzenbaker.
P. 267 D. Tipling/VIREO[T] L. Spitalnik/VIREO[B] **P. 268** Jim Zipp. **P. 269** Jim Zipp. **P. 270** Brian E. Small.
P. 271 Brian E. Small. **P. 272** Brian E. Small. **P. 273** Brian E. Small. **P. 274** Brian E. Small[T]
Mike Danzenbaker[B] **P. 275** Brian E. Small. **P. 276** Brian E. Small. **P. 277** Brian E. Small. **P. 278** Brian E. Small.
P. 279 Garth McElroy[T] Brian E. Small[B] **P. 280** Mike Danzenbaker. **P. 281** Mike Danzenbaker.
P. 282 Brian E. Small. **P. 283** Brian E. Small. **P. 284** Brian E. Small. **P. 285** Brian E. Small. **P. 286** Brian E. Small.
P. 287 Brian E. Small. **P. 288** Brian E. Small. **P. 289** Brian E. Small. **P. 290** Brian E. Small. **P. 291** Brian E. Small.
P. 292 Brian E. Small. **P. 293** Brian E. Small. **P. 294** Brian E. Small. **P. 295** Brian E. Small. **P. 296** Brian E. Small.
P. 297 Brian E. Small. **P. 298** Brian E. Small. **P. 299** Brian E. Small. **P. 300** Brian E. Small. **P. 301** Brian E. Small.
P. 302 Brian E. Small. **P. 303** Brian E. Small. **P. 304** Brian E. Small. **P. 305** Mike Danzenbaker[T]
Brian E. Small[B] **P. 306** R. Curtis/VIREO. **P. 307** Brian E. Small. **P. 308** Brian E. Small. **P. 309** Brian E. Small.
P. 310 Brian E. Small. **P. 311** Brian E. Small. **P. 312** Brian E. Small. **P. 313** Brian E. Small. **P. 314** Brian E. Small.
P. 315 Brian E. Small. **P. 316** Brian E. Small. **P. 317** Jim Zipp. **P. 318** Brian E. Small. **P. 319** Brian E. Small.

Checklist of the Birds of New Jersey

This checklist includes all extant bird species documented as of 2013 in the State of New Jersey. The official state list is maintained by Laurie Larson and Jennifer Hanson of the New Jersey Bird Records Committee. Common names, taxonomy, and sequence of the checklist follow the American Ornithologists' Union (AOU) *Check-list of North American Birds*. Species herein followed by an asterisk (*) are considered rare in New Jersey. These species should be documented with written descriptions and, if possible, photographs, submitted online to the New Jersey Bird Records Committee (njbrc.net).

Family Anatidae:
Ducks, Geese, and Swans
- [ ] Black-bellied Whistling-Duck*
- [ ] Fulvous Whistling-Duck*
- [ ] Pink-footed Goose*
- [ ] Greater White-fronted Goose*
- [ ] Snow Goose
- [ ] Ross's Goose
- [ ] Brant
- [ ] Barnacle Goose*
- [ ] Cackling Goose
- [ ] Canada Goose
- [ ] Mute Swan
- [ ] Tundra Swan
- [ ] Wood Duck
- [ ] Gadwall
- [ ] Eurasian Wigeon
- [ ] American Wigeon
- [ ] American Black Duck
- [ ] Mallard
- [ ] Blue-winged Teal
- [ ] Cinnamon Teal*
- [ ] Northern Shoveler
- [ ] Northern Pintail
- [ ] Garganey*
- [ ] Green-winged Teal
- [ ] Canvasback
- [ ] Redhead
- [ ] Ring-necked Duck
- [ ] Tufted Duck*
- [ ] Greater Scaup
- [ ] Lesser Scaup
- [ ] King Eider
- [ ] Common Eider
- [ ] Harlequin Duck
- [ ] Surf Scoter
- [ ] White-winged Scoter
- [ ] Black Scoter
- [ ] Long-tailed Duck
- [ ] Bufflehead
- [ ] Common Goldeneye
- [ ] Barrow's Goldeneye*
- [ ] Hooded Merganser
- [ ] Common Merganser
- [ ] Red-breasted Merganser
- [ ] Ruddy Duck

Family Odontophoridae:
New World Quails
- [ ] Northern Bobwhite

Family Phasianidae:
Pheasants, Grouse, and Turkeys
- [ ] Ring-necked Pheasant
- [ ] Ruffed Grouse
- [ ] Wild Turkey

Family Gaviidae: Loons
- [ ] Red-throated Loon
- [ ] Pacific Loon*
- [ ] Common Loon

Family Podicipedidae:
Grebes
- [ ] Pied-billed Grebe
- [ ] Horned Grebe
- [ ] Red-necked Grebe
- [ ] Eared Grebe*
- [ ] Western Grebe*

Family Diomedeidae:
Albatrosses
- [ ] Yellow-nosed Albatross*

Family Procellariidae:
Petrels and Shearwaters
- [ ] Northern Fulmar
- [ ] Black-capped Petrel*
- [ ] Cory's Shearwater
- [ ] Great Shearwater
- [ ] Buller's Shearwater*
- [ ] Sooty Shearwater
- [ ] Manx Shearwater*
- [ ] Audubon's Shearwater*

Family Hydrobatidae:
Storm-Petrels
- [ ] Wilson's Storm-Petrel
- [ ] White-faced Storm-Petrel*
- [ ] Leach's Storm-Petrel*
- [ ] Band-rumped Storm-Petrel*

Family Phaethontidae: Tropicbirds
- ☐ White-tailed Tropicbird*
- ☐ Red-billed Tropicbird*

Family Ciconiidae: Storks
- ☐ Wood Stork*

Family Fregatidae: Frigatebirds
- ☐ Magnificent Frigatebird*

Family Sulidae: Boobies and Gannets
- ☐ Masked Booby*
- ☐ Brown Booby*
- ☐ Northern Gannet

Family Phalacrocoracidae: Cormorants
- ☐ Double-crested Cormorant
- ☐ Great Cormorant

Family Anhingidae: Anhingas
- ☐ Anhinga*

Family Pelecanidae: Pelicans
- ☐ American White Pelican
- ☐ Brown Pelican

Family Ardeidae: Herons
- ☐ American Bittern
- ☐ Least Bittern
- ☐ Great Blue Heron
- ☐ Great Egret
- ☐ Western Reef-Heron*
- ☐ Snowy Egret
- ☐ Little Blue Heron
- ☐ Tricolored Heron
- ☐ Reddish Egret*
- ☐ Cattle Egret
- ☐ Green Heron
- ☐ Black-crowned Night-Heron
- ☐ Yellow-crowned Night-Heron

Family Threskiornithidae: Ibises and Spoonbills
- ☐ White Ibis*
- ☐ Glossy Ibis
- ☐ White-faced Ibis*
- ☐ Roseate Spoonbill*

Family Cathartidae: New World Vultures
- ☐ Black Vulture
- ☐ Turkey Vulture

Family Pandionidae: Osprey
- ☐ Osprey

Family Accipitridae: Kites, Hawks, and Eagles
- ☐ Swallow-tailed Kite
- ☐ White-tailed Kite*
- ☐ Mississippi Kite
- ☐ Bald Eagle
- ☐ Northern Harrier
- ☐ Sharp-shinned Hawk
- ☐ Cooper's Hawk
- ☐ Northern Goshawk
- ☐ Red-shouldered Hawk
- ☐ Broad-winged Hawk
- ☐ Swainson's Hawk*
- ☐ Red-tailed Hawk
- ☐ Rough-legged Hawk
- ☐ Golden Eagle

Family Rallidae: Rails and Coots
- ☐ Yellow Rail*
- ☐ Black Rail
- ☐ Corn Crake*
- ☐ Clapper Rail
- ☐ King Rail
- ☐ Virginia Rail
- ☐ Sora
- ☐ Purple Gallinule*
- ☐ Common Gallinule
- ☐ American Coot

Family Gruidae: Cranes
- ☐ Sandhill Crane

Family Recurvirostridae: Avocets and Stilts
- ☐ Black-necked Stilt
- ☐ American Avocet

Family Haematopodidae: Oystercatchers
- ☐ American Oystercatcher

Family Charadriidae: Plovers
- ☐ Northern Lapwing*
- ☐ Black-bellied Plover
- ☐ American Golden-Plover
- ☐ Pacific Golden-Plover*
- ☐ Lesser Sand-Plover*
- ☐ Wilson's Plover*
- ☐ Semipalmated Plover
- ☐ Piping Plover
- ☐ Killdeer

Family Scolopacidae: Sandpipers
- ☐ Spotted Sandpiper
- ☐ Solitary Sandpiper
- ☐ Spotted Redshank*
- ☐ Greater Yellowlegs
- ☐ Willet
- ☐ Lesser Yellowlegs
- ☐ Upland Sandpiper
- ☐ Whimbrel
- ☐ Long-billed Curlew*
- ☐ Black-tailed Godwit*
- ☐ Hudsonian Godwit
- ☐ Bar-tailed Godwit*
- ☐ Marbled Godwit
- ☐ Ruddy Turnstone
- ☐ Red Knot
- ☐ Ruff*
- ☐ Sharp-tailed Sandpiper*
- ☐ Stilt Sandpiper
- ☐ Curlew Sandpiper*
- ☐ Red-necked Stint*
- ☐ Sanderling
- ☐ Dunlin
- ☐ Purple Sandpiper
- ☐ Baird's Sandpiper
- ☐ Little Stint*
- ☐ Least Sandpiper

☐ White-rumped Sandpiper
☐ Buff-breasted Sandpiper
☐ Pectoral Sandpiper
☐ Semipalmated Sandpiper
☐ Western Sandpiper
☐ Short-billed Dowitcher
☐ Long-billed Dowitcher
☐ Wilson's Snipe
☐ Eurasian Woodcock*
☐ American Woodcock
☐ Wilson's Phalarope
☐ Red-necked Phalarope
☐ Red Phalarope

Family Stercorariidae: Skuas and Jaegers

☐ Great Skua*
☐ South Polar Skua*
☐ Pomarine Jaeger
☐ Parasitic Jaeger
☐ Long-tailed Jaeger

Family Alcidae: Auks

☐ Dovekie
☐ Common Murre*
☐ Thick-billed Murre*
☐ Razorbill
☐ Black Guillemot*
☐ Long-billed Murrelet*
☐ Atlantic Puffin

Family Laridae: Gulls, Terns, and Skimmers

☐ Black-legged Kittiwake
☐ Ivory Gull*
☐ Sabine's Gull*
☐ Bonaparte's Gull
☐ Black-headed Gull
☐ Little Gull
☐ Ross's Gull*
☐ Laughing Gull
☐ Franklin's Gull*
☐ Black-tailed Gull*
☐ Mew Gull*
☐ Ring-billed Gull
☐ California Gull*
☐ Herring Gull

☐ Thayer's Gull*
☐ Iceland Gull
☐ Lesser Black-backed Gull
☐ Glaucous Gull
☐ Great Black-backed Gull
☐ Brown Noddy*
☐ Sooty Tern*
☐ Bridled Tern
☐ Least Tern
☐ Large-billed Tern*
☐ Gull-billed Tern
☐ Caspian Tern
☐ Black Tern
☐ White-winged Tern*
☐ Whiskered Tern*
☐ Roseate Tern
☐ Common Tern
☐ Arctic Tern*
☐ Forster's Tern
☐ Royal Tern
☐ Sandwich Tern
☐ Elegant Tern*
☐ Black Skimmer

Family Columbidae: Pigeons and Doves

☐ Rock Pigeon
☐ Band-tailed Pigeon*
☐ Eurasian Collared-Dove*
☐ White-winged Dove*
☐ Mourning Dove
☐ Common Ground-Dove*

Family Cuculidae: Cuckoos

☐ Yellow-billed Cuckoo
☐ Black-billed Cuckoo
☐ Groove-billed Ani*

Family Tytonidae: Barn Owls

☐ Barn Owl

Family Strigidae: Typical Owls

☐ Eastern Screech-Owl
☐ Great Horned Owl
☐ Snowy Owl
☐ Northern Hawk Owl*
☐ Barred Owl

☐ Long-eared Owl
☐ Short-eared Owl
☐ Boreal Owl*
☐ Northern Saw-whet Owl

Family Caprimulgidae: Nightjars

☐ Lesser Nighthawk*
☐ Common Nighthawk
☐ Chuck-will's-widow
☐ Eastern Whip-poor-will

Family Apodidae: Swifts

☐ Black Swift*
☐ Chimney Swift

Family Trochilidae: Hummingbirds

☐ Green Violetear*
☐ Ruby-throated Hummingbird
☐ Black-chinned Hummingbird*
☐ Broad-tailed Hummingbird*
☐ Rufous Hummingbird*
☐ Allen's Hummingbird*
☐ Calliope Hummingbird*

Family Alcedinidae: Kingfishers

☐ Belted Kingfisher

Family Picidae: Woodpeckers

☐ Red-headed Woodpecker
☐ Red-bellied Woodpecker
☐ Yellow-bellied Sapsucker
☐ Downy Woodpecker
☐ Hairy Woodpecker
☐ Red-cockaded Woodpecker*
☐ American Three-toed Woodpecker*
☐ Black-backed Woodpecker*
☐ Northern Flicker
☐ Pileated Woodpecker

Family Falconidae: Caracaras and Falcons

☐ Crested Caracara*
☐ Eurasian Kestrel*
☐ American Kestrel
☐ Merlin
☐ Gyrfalcon*
☐ Peregrine Falcon

Family Psittacidae: Parrots

☐ Monk Parakeet

Family Tryannidae: Tyrant Flycatchers

☐ Olive-sided Flycatcher
☐ Eastern Wood-Pewee
☐ Yellow-bellied Flycatcher
☐ Acadian Flycatcher
☐ Alder Flycatcher
☐ Willow Flycatcher
☐ Least Flycatcher
☐ Eastern Phoebe
☐ Say's Phoebe*
☐ Vermilion Flycatcher*
☐ Ash-throated Flycatcher*
☐ Great Crested Flycatcher
☐ Western Kingbird
☐ Eastern Kingbird
☐ Gray Kingbird*
☐ Scissor-tailed Flycatcher*
☐ Fork-tailed Flycatcher*

Family Laniidae: Shrikes

☐ Loggerhead Shrike*
☐ Northern Shrike

Family Vireonidae: Vireos

☐ White-eyed Vireo
☐ Bell's Vireo*
☐ Yellow-throated Vireo
☐ Cassin's Vireo*
☐ Blue-headed Vireo
☐ Warbling Vireo
☐ Philadelphia Vireo
☐ Red-eyed Vireo

Family Corvidae: Jays and Crows

☐ Blue Jay
☐ American Crow
☐ Fish Crow
☐ Common Raven

Family Alaudidae: Larks

☐ Horned Lark

Family Hirundinidae: Swallows

☐ Purple Martin
☐ Brown-chested Martin*
☐ Tree Swallow
☐ Violet-green Swallow*
☐ Northern Rough-winged Swallow
☐ Bank Swallow
☐ Cliff Swallow
☐ Cave Swallow
☐ Barn Swallow

Family Paridae: Titmice

☐ Carolina Chickadee
☐ Black-capped Chickadee
☐ Boreal Chickadee*
☐ Tufted Titmouse

Family Sittidae: Nuthatches

☐ Red-breasted Nuthatch
☐ White-breasted Nuthatch
☐ Brown-headed Nuthatch*

Family Certhiidae: Treecreepers

☐ Brown Creeper

Family Troglodytidae: Wrens

☐ Rock Wren*
☐ House Wren
☐ Winter Wren
☐ Sedge Wren
☐ Marsh Wren
☐ Carolina Wren
☐ Bewick's Wren*

Family Polioptilidae: Gnatcatchers

☐ Blue-gray Gnatcatcher

Family Regulidae: Kinglets

☐ Golden-crowned Kinglet
☐ Ruby-crowned Kinglet

Family Muscicapidae: Chats

☐ Northern Wheatear*

Family Turdidae: Thrushes

☐ Eastern Bluebird
☐ Mountain Bluebird*
☐ Townsend's Solitaire*
☐ Veery
☐ Gray-cheeked Thrush
☐ Bicknell's Thrush
☐ Swainson's Thrush
☐ Hermit Thrush
☐ Wood Thrush
☐ American Robin
☐ Varied Thrush*

Family Mimidae: Mimic Thrushes

☐ Gray Catbird
☐ Brown Thrasher
☐ Sage Thrasher*
☐ Northern Mockingbird

Family Sturnidae: Starlings

☐ European Starling

Family Motacillidae: Wagtails and Pipits

☐ American Pipit

Family Bombycillidae: Waxwings

☐ Bohemian Waxwing*
☐ Cedar Waxwing

**Family Calcariidae:
Longspurs and
Snow Buntings**

- ☐ Lapland Longspur
- ☐ Chestnut-collared
  Longspur*
- ☐ Smith's Longspur*
- ☐ Snow Bunting

**Family Parulidae:
Wood-Warblers**

- ☐ Ovenbird
- ☐ Worm-eating Warbler
- ☐ Louisiana Waterthrush
- ☐ Northern Waterthrush
- ☐ Golden-winged Warbler
- ☐ Blue-winged Warbler
- ☐ Black-and-white Warbler
- ☐ Prothonotary Warbler
- ☐ Swainson's Warbler*
- ☐ Tennessee Warbler
- ☐ Orange-crowned
  Warbler
- ☐ Nashville Warbler
- ☐ Virginia's Warbler*
- ☐ Connecticut Warbler
- ☐ MacGillivray's Warbler*
- ☐ Mourning Warbler
- ☐ Kentucky Warbler
- ☐ Common Yellowthroat
- ☐ Hooded Warbler
- ☐ American Redstart
- ☐ Cape May Warbler
- ☐ Cerulean Warbler
- ☐ Northern Parula
- ☐ Magnolia Warbler
- ☐ Bay-breasted Warbler
- ☐ Blackburnian Warbler
- ☐ Yellow Warbler
- ☐ Chestnut-sided Warbler
- ☐ Blackpoll Warbler
- ☐ Black-throated Blue
  Warbler
- ☐ Palm Warbler
- ☐ Pine Warbler
- ☐ Yellow-rumped Warbler

- ☐ Yellow-throated Warbler
- ☐ Prairie Warbler
- ☐ Black-throated Gray
  Warbler*
- ☐ Townsend's Warbler*
- ☐ Black-throated Green
  Warbler
- ☐ Canada Warbler
- ☐ Wilson's Warbler
- ☐ Yellow-breasted Chat

**Family Emberizidae:
Sparrows and Buntings**

- ☐ Green-tailed Towhee*
- ☐ Spotted Towhee*
- ☐ Eastern Towhee
- ☐ Cassin's Sparrow*
- ☐ Bachman's Sparrow*
- ☐ American Tree Sparrow
- ☐ Chipping Sparrow
- ☐ Clay-colored Sparrow
- ☐ Field Sparrow
- ☐ Vesper Sparrow
- ☐ Lark Sparrow
- ☐ Black-throated Sparrow*
- ☐ Lark Bunting*
- ☐ Savannah Sparrow
- ☐ Grasshopper Sparrow
- ☐ Henslow's Sparrow*
- ☐ Le Conte's Sparrow*
- ☐ Nelson's Sparrow
- ☐ Saltmarsh Sparrow
- ☐ Seaside Sparrow
- ☐ Fox Sparrow
- ☐ Song Sparrow
- ☐ Lincoln's Sparrow
- ☐ Swamp Sparrow
- ☐ White-throated Sparrow
- ☐ Harris's Sparrow*
- ☐ White-crowned Sparrow
- ☐ Golden-crowned
  Sparrow*
- ☐ Dark-eyed Junco

**Family Cardinalidae:
Tanagers, Grosbeaks,
and Buntings**

- ☐ Summer Tanager
- ☐ Scarlet Tanager
- ☐ Western Tanager*
- ☐ Northern Cardinal
- ☐ Rose-breasted Grosbeak
- ☐ Black-headed Grosbeak*
- ☐ Blue Grosbeak
- ☐ Lazuli Bunting*
- ☐ Indigo Bunting
- ☐ Painted Bunting*
- ☐ Dickcissel

**Family Icteridae:
Blackbirds**

- ☐ Bobolink
- ☐ Red-winged Blackbird
- ☐ Eastern Meadowlark
- ☐ Western Meadowlark*
- ☐ Yellow-headed Blackbird
- ☐ Rusty Blackbird
- ☐ Brewer's Blackbird*
- ☐ Common Grackle
- ☐ Boat-tailed Grackle
- ☐ Brown-headed Cowbird
- ☐ Orchard Oriole
- ☐ Bullock's Oriole*
- ☐ Baltimore Oriole

**Family Fringillidae:
Finches**

- ☐ Brambling*
- ☐ Pine Grosbeak*
- ☐ House Finch
- ☐ Purple Finch
- ☐ Red Crossbill
- ☐ White-winged Crossbill
- ☐ Common Redpoll
- ☐ Hoary Redpoll*
- ☐ Pine Siskin
- ☐ American Goldfinch
- ☐ Evening Grosbeak

**Family Passeridae:
Old World Sparrows**

- ☐ House Sparrow

Species Index

Quick Index

See the Species Index for a complete listing of all birds
in the *ABA Guide to Birds of New Jersey*.